# EVERYDAY GUIDES
# MADE EASY

# CODING
# JAVASCRIPT
# BASICS

This is a FLAME TREE Book
First published 2015

Publisher and Creative Director: Nick Wells
Project Editor: Polly Prior
**Art Director:** Mike Spender
**Layout Design:** Jane Ashley
**Digital Design and Production:** Chris Herbert
**Copy Editor:** Katharine Baker
**Technical Editor:** Chris Brown
**Proofreader:** Dawn Laker
**Indexer:** Helen Snaith
**Screenshots:** Adam Crute
**Picture Research:** Gillian Whitaker

**Special thanks to:** Laura Bulbeck and Josie Mitchell

This edition first published 2015 by
**FLAME TREE PUBLISHING**
6 Melbray Mews
London SW6 3NS
United Kingdom

www.flametreepublishing.com

© 2015 Flame Tree Publishing

ISBN 978-1-78361-418-9

A CIP record for this book is available from the British Library upon request.

Printed in China

All non-screenshot pictures are courtesy of Shutterstock and © the following photographers: Raywoo 5; Dragon Images 6, 117; Morrowind 7, 25, 46; isak55 8, 55; bikeriderlondon 12; Jane Kelly 13, 15; gdainti 13, 15; pogonici 21; Pavel Ignatov 22, 62; Photobank gallery 28; McIek 29, 45, 80; Katharina Wittfeld 33; Pressmaster 36; StockLite 38; Goodluz 43; Matej Kastelic 51; scyther5 52; ronstik 58; wongwean 78; mimagephotography 81; patpitchaya 84, 108; Gwoeii 90; Pixza Studio 91; ra2studio 95; Lincoln Rogers 102; spaxiax 115; NicoElNino 121.

## EVERYDAY GUIDES MADE EASY

# CODING JAVASCRIPT BASICS

ADAM CRUTE

SERIES FOREWORD BY CHRIS BROWN

FLAME TREE
PUBLISHING

# CONTENTS

# SERIES FOREWORD

Imagine you've just invented a language. It isn't much like Java, and you don't plan to use it for scripting. So you call it JavaScript. But this strangely-named language is so ubiquitous in the World Wide Web that you'd be hard pressed to find a web page that doesn't use it. Along with HTML, Style sheets, SQL and a server-side language like C# or VB, it's one of many technologies you need to master to deliver engaging web content to the user. Being a web developer is a big ask.

This book provides a highly accessible introduction to JavaScript, suitable for readers who have no previous programming experience. Building steadily in complexity, and never overwhelming the reader with excessive detail, it covers all the major language features – variables, loops, branches, functions, objects and so on, and introduces the Document Object Model – the formal model that specifies how a web page is represented, and how your JavaScript code can manipulate it before it is presented to the user.

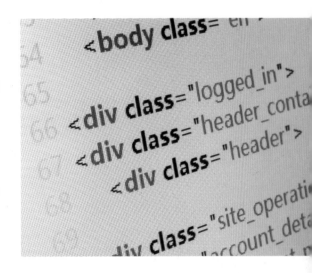

This is not a big book and you'll read it in a few hours. But you'll come out the end knowing enough of the language to build your own interactive web pages.

But don't take my word for it ... turn the page.

**Chris Brown**
**Linux Ambassador and Training Consultant**

# INTRODUCTION

**The JavaScript language has been with us since the very earliest days of the World Wide Web. In its early days it was merely one face in a crowd, one of many languages and technologies vying for the attention and evangelism of the web development community.**

## UNIVERSAL LANGUAGE

Over the years, many such technologies have come into fashion before falling from grace for one reason or another, but not so JavaScript. Thanks largely to a combination of flexibility and

ubiquitousness, JavaScript is now *the* principal scripting language of the internet.

## STEP UP FROM HTML/CSS

Despite JavaScript's at-times esoteric nature, it is the perfect language to use for learning about coding in general. This book is aimed at people who are quite new to programming. You may have spent some time with HTML and CSS and want to step things up with JavaScript, or you may have tinkered with a bit of scripting and want to formalize and expand on that knowledge. You may even be an experienced programmer who has never used JavaScript and wants a quick overview to get started.

## GO-TO PRIMER

There's no getting away from the fact that JavaScript is a deep subject, so much so that no single book can tell you all there is to know about the language. What *this* book aims to do, then, is to deliver a wide-ranging overview of the language, and give you sufficient understanding to be able to add your own simple scripts and interactions to your pages. It is also perfect as a primer for further studies in coding with JavaScript.

## Online Samples

You can download completed versions of all the book's code examples and additional notes. To do so, visit www.flametreepublishing.com/book-samples.html.

## Hot Tips

Look out for the Hot Tips, which tell you about the many shortcuts and quick techniques available in JavaScript.

```
if(parameters.contains(    :name"
    hql += "   and p.name = :name"
}

if(parameters.contains("age
    hql += "   and p.age = :age"
}

TypedQuery<Person> query

if(parameters.contains(
    query.setParameter("na

}

    ters.contain
```

MEET JAVASCRIPT

# JAVASCRIPT, HTML AND CSS

There are three core languages used to develop web pages: HTML provides the underlying structure and content; CSS provides the visual scenery; while JavaScript ...? Well, JavaScript provides the magic that brings the whole thing to life.

## BEFORE WE START

This book is concerned solely with JavaScript, yet the language is so deeply tied to web browsers and web pages that it is impossible to discuss it without relying heavily on prior knowledge of HTML and CSS. If you don't already have such knowledge, the companion to this book, *Coding HTML & CSS Basics*, will kit you out with the requisite know-how.

**EVERYDAY GUIDES**
**MADE EASY**

**CODING HTML & CSS BASICS**

Expert Advice, Made Easy
Website Development • Templates
Font & Style Management

**FLAME TREE PUBLISHING**

Frederic Johnson & Adam Crute

### Hot Tip

If, in the context of HTML and CSS, you understand the meaning of terms such as element, attribute, opening and closing tags, selectors and style rules, you're good to go with JavaScript.

**Left:** Coding HTML & CSS Basics will set you up with the knowledge you need to understand how to code JavaScript.

# BROWSER COMPATIBILITY

While the core JavaScript language is fully supported across all major browsers, problems can arise when using advanced or esoteric functions, because not all browsers support all of JavaScript's extended functionality. There are ways and means to work around such issues but, unfortunately, there isn't room to cover them here.

**Hot Tip**

See page 7 to find out how to download completed versions of all the book's code examples. These files include additional notes that help to further explain the examples.

## Firefox

All of the examples in this book use standard JavaScript programming techniques and constructs. However, in order to sidestep any irksome browser compatibility issues, we'll be using the Firefox browser for running all examples, and encourage you to do the same.

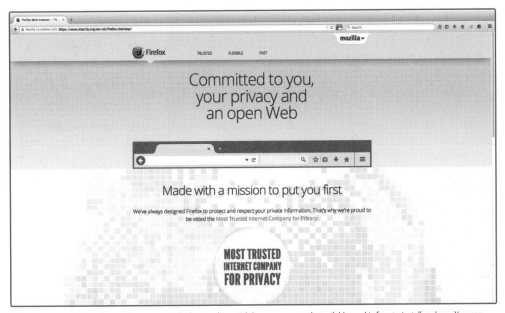

**Above:** Mozilla Firefox is one of the most standards-compliant web browsers currently available, and is free to install and use. You can download it from www.mozilla.org.

# WHAT IS JAVASCRIPT?

JavaScript is a scripting language used to interact with and control pages loaded into a web browser. It provides a rich palette of functionality for interacting with the user, the page and the internet.

## WHAT IS A SCRIPT?

In the theatre world, a script can be thought of as a series of instructions that tell the actors the actors where to be, what to do and say, and when to do and say it. In computing, the meaning is very similar: a script is a series of instructions for the computer to perform. Yes, the actors are onscreen graphics and chunks of data rather than a troupe of thespians, but the principle remains the same.

**Left**: A script tells the actors where to be, what to do and when to do it – the actors being computer data and graphics, of course.

# JAVASCRIPT RUNS ON THE CLIENT SIDE

It's important to understand from the get-go that when using JavaScript in a web page, it runs on the user's – or client's – computer and interacts with a copy of the web page that is loaded into a web browser on that computer. This is often referred to as 'client-side' scripting.

## Java and JavaScript

You may have heard of a language called Java, and think that it somehow relates to JavaScript – it doesn't. Java was a hot topic at the time JavaScript was developed, and by calling the language JavaScript, its developers ensured that it got noticed. Other than a passing similarity in their syntax though, the two languages are fundamentally different and unrelated.

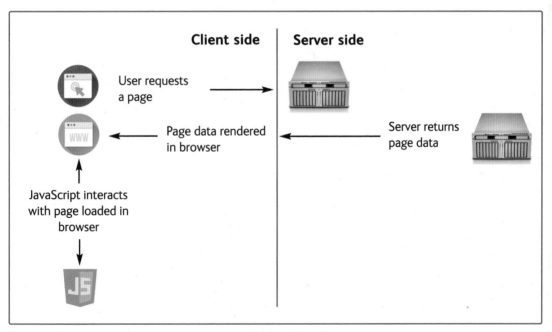

**Above:** JavaScript interacts directly with the page impression that's loaded into the user's browser.

# WHY INCLUDE SCRIPTS IN A PAGE?

There are almost as many reasons for using scripting in a page as there are pages that use scripting. In general though, there are two key reasons for using scripts: to modify the appearance of a page; and/or to allow communication between a page and a web server.

## VISUAL CHANGES

Some of the most common – certainly the most obvious – scripts modify the appearance of a page based upon conditions that weren't known when the page was authored. A condition could be as simple as the time of day or the position of the user's mouse pointer, or it could be very complex. The point is that by using JavaScript, we can determine whether a certain condition has been met and then take action in response to that condition.

**Right:** Search engines use scripting to display possible search results as you type.

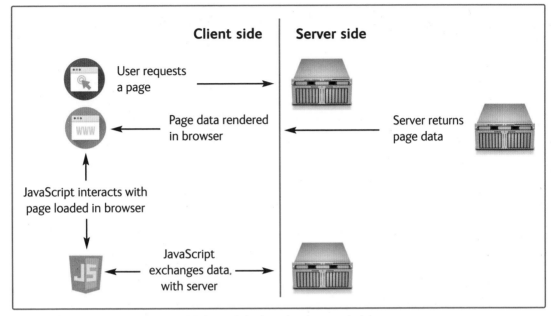

**Above:** JavaScript can pull data from a server and display it in the browser without having to reload the page.

# COMMUNICATIONS

There are many scenarios in which a loaded page can require additional data from a server. For instance, many search engines pop up a list of suggestions while you type into the search field – getting the list is done via scripted communications between the browser and server.

**Above:** Google Analytics uses scripting extensively to pass data between a page in a browser and Google's servers.

## Working Behind the Scenes

Not all scripts result in visual output – a perfect example being Google Analytics. This script monitors various metrics about visits (and visitors) to a page: total visits, unique visits, geographic location of visitors, and so on. JavaScript ships this data back to Google's servers, from where the page's owner can view and analyse the data.

# WRITING JAVASCRIPT

As with HTML and CSS, JavaScript is plain text. This means that the simplest tool for writing JavaScript is the basic text editor built into your computer's operating system (Notepad on Windows, TextEdit on a Mac or Vi on Linux).

## IDEs

Plain text editors work fine, but they pale into insignificance compared to a fully fledged **IDE** (integrated development environment). IDEs help both with writing scripts – speeding up your work and helping to spot errors – and with managing the multitude of files associated with a website or larger project.

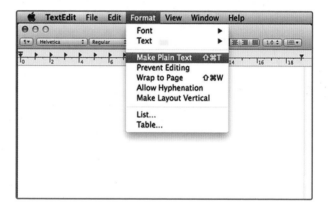

**Above:** JavaScript has to be written in plain text files – don't use Rich Text!

### Popular Cross-Platform IDEs

○ **Adobe Dreamweaver**: When it comes to developing for the web, Dreamweaver is the daddy. It's also the daddy price-wise, especially given Adobe's controversial subscription-only licensing model. Weigh up your options wisely. www.adobe.com

## Hot Tip

If using TextEdit on a Mac as your JavaScript editor, be sure to switch all new documents to plain text mode before typing anything.

- **Komodo IDE:** This fully featured commercial IDE costs $99/£67.75 for a single licence (at the time of writing) and is very popular, thanks to its clean, uncluttered interface and slick operation. http://komodoide.com

- **Komodo Edit:** The cut-down version of Komodo IDE is free to download and use, and is an excellent choice for exploring the benefits of an IDE. http://komodoide.com/komodo-edit/

- **Eclipse:** This powerful IDE can work with many different languages, including HTML, CSS and JavaScript. It is free to download and use, but can be overwhelming for the uninitiated. www.eclipse.org

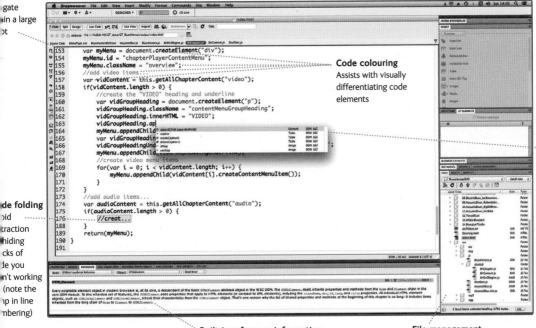

mbering
s us to
gate
in a large
ot

Code colouring
Assists with visually
differentiating code
elements

Code hinting
Shows a context-sensitive list of possible functions, methods and properties as you type

de folding
oid
traction
hiding
cks of
de you
n't working
(note the
p in line
mbering)

Built-in reference information
Some IDEs include language reference information

File management
Built-in file management features are invaluable with larger projects

**Above:** IDEs provide many useful features for the developer.

# ADDING A SCRIPT TO A PAGE

We add scripts to a page by using the `<script>` HTML element. The `type` attribute of the element must always be `"text/javascript"`. The element should always be closed with a closing tag, `</script>`.

## Embedded JavaScript

To embed a script, we simply write its commands between the opening and closing `<script>` tags. The script is then intrinsically tied to that page, and that page alone.

```
1  <!DOCTYPE HTML>
2  <html>
3      <head>
4          <meta charset="UTF-8">
5          <title>Untitled Document</title>
6
7          <script type="text/javascript">
8              //Embedded JavaScript code here
9          </script>
10
11         <script type="text/javascript" src="js/myScript.js"></script>
12
13      </head>
14
15      <body>
16      </body>
17  </html>
```

**Above:** The HTML `<script>` element can contain an embedded script or link to an external script file.

**Left:** Store your scripts in a subfolder of your website — js is a good name for this folder.

## Linked JavaScript

It is common to link a script to a page. To do this, the script is written in a separate text file and saved with a *.js* filename extension. The script is then linked to a page using the `src` attribute of the `<script>` element.

For example:

```
<script
type="text/javascript"
src="myScript.js"></script>
```

# WHAT HAPPENS WHEN A BROWSER ENCOUNTERS A SCRIPT?

Whenever a web browser loads a page, it deals with each HTML element sequentially as it works through the page.

## THE INTERPRETER

When the browser encounters a `<script type="text/javascript">` element, the contents of the script are immediately passed to the browser's JavaScript **interpreter** (known as executing the script). It is the interpreter's job to make sense of the script and instruct the browser to act accordingly. When the interpreter has finished executing a script, control is returned to the browser, which then continues to process the page.

```
1   <!DOCTYPE HTML>
2   <html>
3       <head>
4           <title>A Simple Quiz</title>
5
6           <script type="text/javascript" src="js/QuizQuestion.js"></script>
7           <script type="text/javascript" src="js/SimpleQuiz.js"></script>
8           <script type="text/javascript" src="js/quizStartup.js"></script>
9
10      </head>
11
12      <body>
13
14
15      </body>
16  </html>
17
```

```
1   //Declare a namespace
2   var com;
3   if(!com) {
4       com = {};
5   }
6   if(!com.flametreepublishing) {
7       com.flametreepublishing = {};
8   }
9
10  //Define the constructor function - this we'll
11  //place in our namespace so as not to pollute
12  //the global namespace
13  com.flametreepublishing.QuizQuestion = function(aQuestionNum, aQuestionText, aAnswers, aCorrectAnswerIndex) {
14      //The initial parameters for the question have been provided to the constructor
15      //We store them in the instance using the 'this' keyword
16      this.questionNum = aQuestionNum;
17      this.questionText = aQuestionText;
18      this.answers = aAnswers;
19      this.correctAnswerIndex = aCorrectAnswerIndex;
20  }
21
22  com.flametreepublishing.QuizQuestion.prototype.checkUserAnswer = function(answerIndex) {
23      //Create a variable to store the result of the method
24      var theResult;
25      //compare the answerIndex value to this.correctAnswerIndex
26      if(answerIndex == this.correctAnswerIndex) {
27          theResult = true;
28      } else {
```

**Right:** JavaScript is processed in-place as the page loads.

# YOUR FIRST SCRIPT

1. Create a new HTML file and add the basic structural elements `<html>`, `<head>` and `<body>`. Save the file in a convenient location, and call it myFirstScript.html.

2. Add a <script> element to the <body> element. For this example, we want to place the opening and closing tags on separate lines, with an empty line in between.

3. Type the following command within the script element: `document.write("<p>Hello World!</p>");`. This command outputs text to a page, just as though we'd typed it directly into the page (which is why we've also included the `<p>` element tags).

4. Save the page and then open it in Firefox, either by double-clicking the file or by right-clicking it and selecting Open with, then Firefox.

**Hot Tip**

We often use the terms 'code' and 'coding' – the former refers to the text that you type into a script, while the latter refers to the process of writing scripts.

```
1   <!DOCTYPE HTML>
2   <html>
3       <head>
4           <title>My First Script</title>
5       </head>
6
7       <body>
8
9           <script type="text/javascript">
10              document.write("<p>Hello World!</p>");
11          </script>
12
13      </body>
14  </html>
15
```

**Right:** Greetings, JavaScript!

## How it Works

Congratulations — you've just written and executed your first script. The script was passed to the interpreter when the browser encountered the `<script>` element. The interpreter recognized the `document.write` command, and wrote the text contained in the brackets (or, in programming parlance, **parentheses**) to the page. The text had to be contained in quotation marks for the interpreter to recognize it as text — if all you see is a blank page, chances are you've missed the quotation marks.

# Hot Tip

It is traditional for books about programming languages to use "Hello World!" as the output from the first exercise in the book — you are now officially initiated into the ranks of the developer!

**Right:** You have passed the initiation test — welcome aboard!

DATA IN JAVASCRIPT

# WHAT IS DATA?

A key concept in all programming languages is data. Data can be thought of as any piece of information that is used within a program.

## ALL DATA HAS A VALUE

Any piece of data can be said to have a **value**. This value can be simple – for example, a number or a paragraph of text – or it can be complex, such as a list of numbers or many paragraphs. Whatever the type of data, though, the information being represented by that data is referred to as the data's value.

### Literals

A **literal** is a piece of data with a specific value that's typed directly into a script. The following are all examples of literals: `"Hello World"`, `true`, `42` and `null`.

### Identifiers

An **identifier** is a case sensitive name that's assigned to a piece of data (or to a function – *see* Named Functions on page 81). Once assigned, an identifier can be used to refer to that data (or function) within a script. JavaScript leaves you free to choose the names you wish to use as identifiers, as long as you follow a few basic rules.

```
3
4  myNumberLiteral = 42;
5  myStringLiteral = "Hello World";
6  myBooleanLiteral = true;
7  myNullLiteral = null;
8
```

**Above:** Literal values are typed directly into a script.

## Identifier Naming Rules

○ **Reserved words:**
JavaScript defines a number of words that have special meaning for the language (*see* page 50). These can't be used as names for your own identifiers.

○ **First character:** The first character of an identifier must be a letter, an underscore '_' or a dollar '$'.

○ **Subsequent characters:** The remaining characters in an identifier can only be letters, numbers, underscores or dollars.

**Right:** The first set of identifiers are all legal (in other words, allowed) identifiers, while the second set are illegal.

```
1  //Examples of legal identifiers
2  myValue
3  _myValue
4  MY_VALUE
5  $myvalue
6  my$Value23
7  my_$_value_23
8
9  //Examples of illegal identifiers
10 23myvalue
11 myValue*
12 my-value
13 #myvalue
14 my%value
15 my¢Value
16
```

# VARIABLES

In essence, a variable is a portion of computer memory that's used for storing data, and which is referred to using an identifier.

## DECLARING A VARIABLE

It's very easy to declare a new variable in JavaScript – all we do is write the keyword `var` followed by the identifier we want to use to refer to the variable. For example:

`var theAnswer;`

**Assigning a Value to a Variable**

It is common to assign a value to a variable at the time it is declared, like this:

```
 4  //Declaring variables (without and with assignment)
 5  var theQuestion;
 6  var theAnswer = 42;
 7
 8  //Assigning a value to a declared variable
 9  theQuestion = "Life, the Universe and Everything";
10
```

**Above:** Variables are easy to declare and use.

`var theAnswer = 42;`

**Changing the Value of a Variable**

Once a variable has been declared with `var`, we can change the value assigned to it like this: `theAnswer = 54`. Notice that we didn't include the `var` keyword this time.

### Hot Tip

In JavaScript, = does not mean equals – it means assignment (*see* page 56).

## Getting the Value of a Variable

To use the value stored in a variable, we write that variable's identifier name in the place where we need to use the value.

1. Create a new HTML document and add the common structural elements (`<html>`, `<head>` and `<body>`). Save the document as gettingVariables.html.

2. Add a `<script type="text/javascript">` element as a child of (i.e. within) the `<body>` element, as shown below.

3. Add the JavaScript code shown below.

4. Save your work and then open the file in Firefox.

```
1   <!DOCTYPE HTML>
2   <html>
3       <head>
4           <title>Getting Variables</title>
5       </head>
6
7       <body>
8
9           <script type="text/javascript">
10
11          </script>
12
13      </body>
14  </html>
```

**Above:** Step 2: Add a `<script type="text/javascript">` element.

```
10          <script type="text/javascript">
11              var theMessage = "The alert function displays a message in a dialog box.";
12              alert(theMessage);
13              theMessage = "Here we're just changing a variable's value...";
14              alert(theMessage);
15              theMessage = "...and passing that variable's identifier to the alert function.";
16              alert(theMessage);
17              theMessage = "The interpreter then looks up the variable's value...";
18              alert(theMessage);
19              theMessage = "...and that's what we see in the dialog box. Simple, eh?";
20              alert(theMessage);
21          </script>
```

**Above:** Step 3: Add the JavaScript code.

**Above:** Computer data is simply numbers.

## DATA MECHANICS

Unlike lower-level programming languages such as C and Java, JavaScript does not require the programmer to get involved in the details of how data is stored on the computer – the interpreter manages such intricacies for us.

However, you should still appreciate that everything your computer does – every email you write, every song you listen to, every video you watch – is represented by numbers. Therefore, at the most fundamental level, all computer data is just numbers.

### Hot Tip

The binary and hexadecimal number systems are intrinsically tied to the way computers represent numbers and data – look them up on Wikipedia if you don't know how they work.

# DATA TYPES

**All data handled by JavaScript has a data type. This specifies the nature of the data being handled – whether it's a number, text, a list and so on.**

## WHAT IS A DATA TYPE?

In order to translate a piece of data into anything useful, a computer or program has to know what the data is intended to represent – it has to know the type of the data. Because data is stored in variables, we normally refer to variables as having a data type, or as being of type so and so. Data types fall into two groups: primitive and reference. Let's take a look at what that means.

**Above:** Data types define the meaning of the raw numbers stored by a computer.

# PRIMITIVE AND REFERENCE DATA TYPES

**Primitive** data types can be thought of as those whose data represents a single value, such as a number, while **reference** data types represent complex data, such as a list.

When a variable of a primitive type is used in a script, the interpreter copies the variable's value and uses this copy in its calculations. In contrast, when a variable of reference type is used, the interpreter works directly with the data stored in memory.

**Primitive data type**

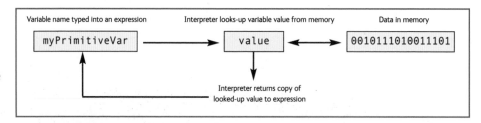

**Reference data type**

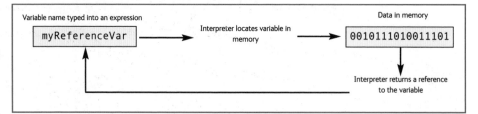

**Above:** Primitive data types return a copy of their in-memory value; reference types return a direct reference to their in-memory value.

## Understanding the Difference Between Primitive and Reference Data Types

1. Create a new HTML document containing the common structural elements (`<html>`, `<head>` and `<body>`). Save the file as datatypes.html.

> ## Hot Tip
> **From now on, we won't tell you which common elements to add to a basic HTML document – you know by now.**

2. Create a `<script>` element as a child of (i.e. within) the `<body>` element, being sure to set the `type` attribute to `"text/javascript"`, as shown below).

```
1  <!DOCTYPE HTML>
2  <html>
3      <head>
4          <title>Exploring Primitive and Reference Datatypes</title>
5      </head>
6
7      <body>
8          <script type="text/javascript">
9
10         </script>
11
12     </body>
13 </html>
```

**Above:** Step 2.

```
8          <script type="text/javascript">
9              document.write("<h2>PRIMITIVE DATATYPES </h2>");
10             var primitiveVar1 = 72;
11             var primitiveVar2 = primitiveVar1;
12             document.write("<p>primitiveVar1 has value " + primitiveVar1 + "</p>");
13             document.write("<p>primitiveVar2 has value " + primitiveVar2 + "</p>");
14             var primitiveVar2 = 12;
15             document.write("<p>primitiveVar1 now has value " + primitiveVar1 + "</p>");
16             document.write("<p>primitiveVar2 now has value " + primitiveVar2 + "</p>");
17         </script>
18
```

**Above:** Step 3: Enter this code into your new `<script>` element.

3. Enter the code shown above within this new `script` element.

4. Save your work and then open datatypes.html in Firefox.

5. As you can see, even though we assigned `primitiveVar1` to `primitiveVar2`, the value of `primitiveVar1` did not change when we changed the value of `primitiveVar2`. In other words, each variable references an independent value.

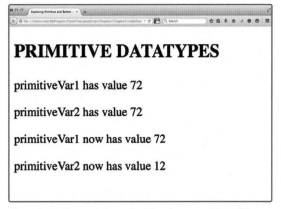

# PRIMITIVE DATATYPES

primitiveVar1 has value 72

primitiveVar2 has value 72

primitiveVar1 now has value 72

primitiveVar2 now has value 12

**Above:** Step 5: The script's output shows how the two variables are behaving.

```
14    var primitiveVar2 = 12;
15    document.write("<p>primitiveVar1 now has value " + primitiveVar1 + "</p>");
16    document.write("<p>primitiveVar2 now has value " + primitiveVar2 + "</p>");
17
18    document.write("<h2>REFERENCE DATATYPES </h2>");
19    var referenceVar1 = {};
20    referenceVar1.myValue = 72;
21    var referenceVar2 = referenceVar1;
22    document.write("<p>referenceVar1.myValue has value " + referenceVar1.myValue + "</p>");
23    document.write("<p>referenceVar2.myValue has value " + referenceVar2.myValue + "</p>");
24    referenceVar2.myValue = 12;
25    document.write("<p>referenceVar1.myValue now has value " + referenceVar1.myValue + "</p>");
26    document.write("<p>referenceVar2.myValue now has value " + referenceVar2.myValue + "</p>");
27  </script>
```

**Above:** Step 6: Add this code into your editor.

6. Go back to your editor and add the new code shown above (the old code is dimmed). Here we are using an **object** as a reference data type – these are discussed starting on page 39.

7. Save your work and launch the page in Firefox.

8. Notice how changing the value of `referenceVar2.myValue` also changed the value of `referenceVar1.myValue`. This is because both `referenceVar1` and `referenceVar2` point to the same data in memory, so changing one changes the other, too.

## Know Your Primitive from Your Reference

It is important to keep this distinction in mind – not doing so can lead to some major bugs in your JavaScript applications. The good news is that you will find it becomes second nature very quickly.

```
7    <body>
8        <script type="text/javascript">
9            var playerObjectTemplate = {};
10           var player1 = playerObjectTemplate;
11           player1.playerName = "Sarah";
12           player1.startingScore = 4;
13           var player2 = playerObjectTemplate;
14           player2.playerNcme = "Steven";
15           player2.startingScore = 12;
16           alert(player1.playerName); //Alert box will say "Steven", not "Sarah"
17           alert(player1.startingScore); //Alert box will say 12, not 4
18       </script>
19
20   </body>
```

**Above:** This script won't work as intended because all variables are pointing to the same object – try it and see for yourself.

# THE PRIMITIVE DATA TYPES

Let's take a look at the primitive data types. Remember, variables of these types represent a single value.

## Booleans

Booleans represent a single **bit** of computer data and as such are simplest data type there is. A Boolean can have a value of either `false` or `true`, represented within the computer as 0 or 1 respectively.

## Numbers

Generally, in computing, there are two types of number: integers and floats. The former are whole numbers, and the latter are numbers that involve a fractional or exponential component, such as 3.14 or $0.945\times10^7$. JavaScript doesn't worry itself with such distinctions – a number is a number.

## Strings

Strings are text data – don't worry about why they're called strings (it gets technical in ways we don't need to worry about), just know that a string is text, and text is a string.

When writing strings into scripts, they have to be surrounded by quotation marks. These can be single ' or double " quotes (we'll be using the latter), but it's vital that a string is closed by the same style of quotation mark that it was opened with.

An empty string – a string with no characters in it – is normally written as a pair of quotation marks:

' ' or " ".

> ## Hot Tip
>
> **If a string is enclosed by single quotes ', it can contain double quotes ", and vice versa.**

```
1  <!DOCTYPE HTML>
2  <html>
3      <head>
4          <title>Using Quotes in Strings</title>
5      </head>
6
7      <body>
8          <script type="text/javascript">
9              var anyString = ""; //"" creates an empty string
10             anyString = 'A string can be demarked by single quotes...';
11             anyString = "...or it can be demarked by double quotes.";
12             anyString = 'A string demarked by single quotes "can" contain double quotes';
13             anyString = "A string demarked by double quotes 'can' contain single quotes";
14         </script>
15
16     </body>
17 </html>
18
```

**Above:** Different ways of using quotation marks with strings

## Non-existent Data

JavaScript has two data types for representing non-existent data. The null type, whose value is also null, indicates that there is no value – if an identifier evaluates to null, it doesn't contain any valid data or, most likely, it hasn't been declared. The second type is undefined, whose value is also undefined, and is slightly different to null – it is the initial type and value of any variable that has been declared but not yet had a value assigned to it.

# ARRAYS

**Arrays** are a reference data type; array is JavaScript parlance for a list of values. There are two ways in which to create one.

## Writing an Array Literal

We can create an array by writing an array literal, like this:

```
var myArray = [value_1, value_2, ..., value_n]
```

```
1  <!DOCTYPE HTML>
2  <html>
3      <head>
4          <title>Array Examples</title>
5      </head>
6
7      <body>
8          <script type="text/javascript">
9              var emptyArray = [];
10             var numbersArray = [42, 12, 57, 3.14, 901582, 5];
11             var stringsArray = ["Harry", "Sue", "Julia", "Chris", "Oliver"];
12             var mixedArray = ["Oliver", true, false, 5];
13             var arraysArray = [emptyArray, numbersArray, stringsArray, mixedArray];
14         </script>
15     </body>
16 </html>
```

**Above:** Arrays store lists of other data (including other arrays).

The square brackets [ ] mark the start and end of the array, while the values to store within the array – its **elements** – are separated by commas and can be of any data type. To create an empty array, we just type the brackets with no elements within them.

## Creating an Array with the New Keyword
We can also create an array using the new keyword: var myArray = new Array();. Initial elements, separated by commas, can be included between the parentheses. (We discuss keywords on page 50.)

## Array Length
The number of elements within an array is referred to as its length. If we have an array called myArray, we can get its length by typing myArray.length.

```
1  <!DOCTYPE HTML>
2  <html>
3      <head>
4          <title>Array Examples</title>
5      </head>
6
7      <body>
8          <script type="text/javascript">
9              var userNames = new Array("Helen", "Amrit", "Geoff", "Jacques");
10             var userLogins = new Array();
11             alert(userNames.length) //Displays '4' in the alert dialog
12             alert(userLogins.length) //Displays '0' in the alert dialog
13         </script>
14     </body>
15 </html>
16
```

**Above:** Arrays can be created with the new keyword, and always have a length.

## Accessing Array Elements

Each element in an array has an **index**, this being a number that refers to the position of the element within the array. The first element has an index of 0, the second an index of 1 and so on. To access a specific element of an array, we write the array variable's name followed by the index number wrapped in square brackets. For example, if we want to use the third element (index 2) of the array `myArray`, we write `myArray[2]`.

> ## Hot Tip
>
> **Array elements can contain any data type you like – including other arrays.**

## Adding Elements to an Array

We can also assign values to elements of an array using square brackets. For example, to set the eighth element (index 7) of the array `myArray`, we could type `myArray[7] = 19`. If the eighth element already contains data, it is overwritten with the new value. Or, if the array's length is less than 8, the new element is created, as are any empty elements required to pad between the last element of the unmodified array and the newly added element.

```
 7    <body>
 8        <script type="text/javascript">
 9            var userNames = new Array("Helen", "Amrit", "Geoff", "Jacques");
10            var userLogins = new Array();
11            //Get array element values...:
12            alert(userNames[0]); //Displays 'Helen' in the alert dialog
13            alert(userNames[3]); //Displays 'Jacques' in the alert dialog
14            //Set array element values...:
15            userLogins[0] = ["Amrit", "Monday"]; //Assign array to 1st element of userLogins
16            userLogins[2] = ["Helen", "Tuesday"]; //Assign array to 3rd element of userLogins
17            //Get undeclared array element value...:
18            alert(userLogins[1]);   //Displays 'undefined' in the alert dialog, I.E. the element
19                                    //exists - it was created for us - but it has not had a
20                                    //value assigned to it
21        </script>
22    </body>
```

**Above:** We can access array elements, for both getting and setting a value, using bracket access notation.

## Appending Elements to an Array

The push() method of an array enables us to append elements to the end of that array (we discuss methods on page 102). For example, if we wished to append the string "Harry" to the array firstNames, we could write this as  firstNames.push("Harry").

```
7      <body>
8          <script type="text/javascript">
9              var userNames = new Array("Helen", "Amrit", "Geoff", "Jacques");
10             alert(userNames.length); //Displays '4' in the alert dialog
11             userNames.push("Oliver");
12             alert(userNames.length); //Displays '5' in the alert dialog
13             alert(userNames[4]); //Displays 'Oliver' in the alert dialog
14         </script>
15     </body>
```

**Above:** The push method of an array adds an element to the end of the array.

## Removing Elements from an Array

We can remove the first element in an array using the `shift()` method, or remove the last element using the `pop()` method. Whichever method you use, it will return the value that was removed.

```
7      <body>
8          <script type="text/javascript">
9              var userNames = new Array("Helen", "Amrit", "Geoff", "Jacques");
10             userNames.push("Oliver");
11             alert(userNames.length); //Displays '5' in the alert dialog
12             var firstNameInArray = userNames.shift();
13             alert(firstNameInArray); //Displays 'Helen' in the alert dialog
14             alert(userNames.length); //Displays '4' in the alert dialog
15             var lastNameInArray = userNames.pop();
16             alert(lastNameInArray); //Displays 'Oliver' in the alert dialog
17             alert(userNames.length); //Displays '3' in the alert dialog
18         </script>
19     </body>
```

**Above:** The `shift()` and `pop()` methods of an array remove the first and last elements, respectively.

## Other Array Methods

Arrays have many other methods that we use to manipulate their content – far too many to cover here. For a comprehensive list, visit www.w3schools.com/js/js_array_methods.asp.

# OBJECTS

A variable of type object (a reference data type) is a variable in which we can store multiple values. Unlike the index-based access of an array, however, an object stores values against named **properties** (often called a property-value pair).

Objects have a special role in JavaScript – they are the basic building blocks upon which all other JavaScript data is built. Every other data type inherits its basic characteristics from the object data type. For this reason, we often refer to any and all JavaScript data as being an object – a string object, for example, or an array object. This concept of inheritance is fundamental to object oriented programming, an approach to coding that is closely tied to JavaScript, and that we introduce on page 95.

**Hot Tip**

The values stored in the properties of an object can be of any data type, including other objects or arrays.

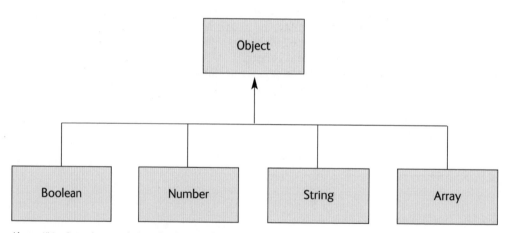

**Above:** All JavaScript objects are built on the object data type.

## Creating an Object

We can create an object either by declaring an object literal, or by using the `new` keyword – let's try both.

1. Create a new HTML document containing the common structural elements. Add a `<script type="text/javascript">` element as the child of the body element, then save the document as javascriptObjects.html.

```
7      <body>
8          <script type="text/javascript">
9              var quizQuestion1 = new Object();
10             quizQuestion1.question = "Approximately how far is the Sun from the Earth?";
11             quizQuestion1.answer = "93,000,000 miles";
12             quizQuestion1.wrongAnswer1 = "200 miles";
13             quizQuestion1.wrongAnswer2 = "49,000,000 miles";
14             quizQuestion1.wrongAnswer3 = "150,000 miles";
15
16         </script>
17     </body>
```

**Above:** Step 2: Enter the code shown here into your HTML document.

2. Enter the code shown in the illustration above. This uses the new keyword to create an empty object, then declares a number of properties on that object.

3. Enter the new code showing in the illustration below, in which we create an object using object literal notation: each property name is followed by a colon and a value; property-value pairs are separated by commas; the whole literal is wrapped in braces (curly brackets { }).

```
13             quizQuestion1.wrongAnswer2 = "49,000,000 miles";
14             quizQuestion1.wrongAnswer3 = "150,000 miles";
15
16             var quizQuestion2 = {
17                 question:"How many planets orbit the Sun?",
18                 answer:"8",
19                 wrongAnswer1:"6",
20                 wrongAnswer2:"7",
21                 wrongAnswer3:"9"
22             };
23
24         </script>
```

**Above:** Step 3: Enter the code highlighted here.

4. Finally, we once again declare an object literal – but this time, it's an empty one that could be used for storing answers to the questions stored in the objects we've created. See the illustration below.

```
15
16                  var quizQuestion2 = {
17                      question:"How many planets orbit the Sun?",
18                      answer:"8",
19                      wrongAnswer1:"6",
20                      wrongAnswer2:"7",
21                      wrongAnswer3:"9"
22                  };
23
24              var userAnswers = {};
25
26          </script>
27      </body>
28 </html>
29
```

**Above:** Step 4: Here, you will create an empty object.

5. Save your work. If you launch this page in Firefox, you won't see any visual output, but that's OK – for now, this is more of a coding and thought exercise, but we will be building on it as we progress.

6. Notice how we've created the same structure of property names within both of the quizQuestion objects – creating and reusing object structures in this way is a key principle in object oriented programming, which we discuss on page 95.

**Hot Tip**

The rules governing property names are the same as those for all identifiers – see page 25.

```
23
24          var userAnswers = {};
25
26
27          alert(quizQuestion1.question);
28          alert(quizQuestion2.question);
29
30      </script>
31    </body>
32  </html>
33
```

**Above:** Accessing the value stored in an object property is very easy.

## Accessing Object Properties

If we have an object, `myObject`, on which we've defined a property, `myProperty`, we can access that property by typing `myObject.myProperty`. The '.' is called the **dot** operator (*see* page 53).

## DATA TYPE CASTING

There are many occasions when you need to use a value of one type in the context of another type. For example, you may wish to use the string representation of a number (`"42"` instead of `42`), or you may need to use a number in the context of a Boolean value. Translating between data types in this way is referred to as data type **casting**.

## Implicit Casting

JavaScript is very proactive when it comes to managing data types, and automatically casts between types depending on the context in which they are being used (*see* page 55 for an example of this).

## Explicit Casting

We can also explicitly cast some data types, most often used when casting between strings and numbers. To cast a number to a string, for example, we would write `String(42)`, giving the result `"42"`. Conversely, to cast a string to a number, we would write `Number("42")`, resulting in 42.

```
1  var myNumber = 42;
2  var myString = "549";
3  var myName = "Sajid";
4
5  var test1 = myNumber + myString;
6  alert(test1); //Shows '42549' in the alert box
7
8  var test2 = myNumber + Number(myString);
9  alert(test2); //Shows '591' in the alert box
10
11 var test3 = myString + myName;
12 alert(test3); //Shows '549Sajid' in the alert box
13
14 var test4 = myNumber + Number(myName);
15 alert(test4); //Shows 'NaN' in the alert box
16
17 var test5 = String(myNumber) + myName;
18 alert(test5); //Shows '42Sajid' in the alert box
19
20
```

**Above:** This code highlights how and why we might explicitly cast between data types.

## The Special NaN Number

Not all values can be converted to a number – for example, the string `"foo"` has no numeric meaning.

If we cast this string to a number, we'd get the result NaN (Not a Number). Despite the name, this is indeed a number, and can be used anywhere that a number is allowed or expected. However, any calculations that include NaN always evaluate to NaN themselves.

## Results of Casting Different Data Types

This table shows the results of casting between different data types. Read the table as 'casting from row title to column title'.

| | Boolean | number | string |
|---|---|---|---|
| Boolean | - | `false` is 0, `true` is 1 | `false` is `"false"`, `true` is `"true"` |
| number | 0 is `false`, else `true` | - | String representation of number |
| string | `""` is `false`, else `true` | numeric representation of string, or NaN | - |
| null | `false` | 0 | `"null"` |
| undefined | `false` | NaN | `"undefined"` |
| array | `true` | Empty array is 0, array with elements is NaN | comma-separated list of element values |
| object | `true` | NaN | `"object Object"` |

```
preg_match($this->SUB_REPL

// a simple lookup? (e.g.

(preg_match($this->INDEXE

// store the index = (int) (subst
$replacement

e { // a complicated looku
// build a function to do t
ote = preg_match($this->OU
? '"' : '";
acement = array(
```

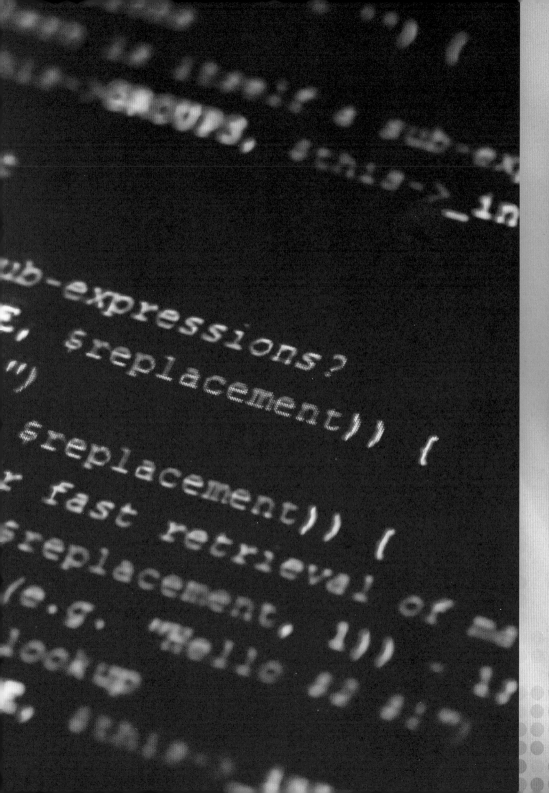

ANATOMY OF JAVASCRIPT

# JAVASCRIPT SYNTAX

A script can consist of a single instruction or it can be an epic tome containing thousands of lines of code. No matter the size though, all scripts in JavaScript share a common structure and syntax.

## CASE SENSITIVITY

The first thing to note is that JavaScript is case sensitive, i.e. lower-case characters are considered to be distinct from their upper-case counterparts. For example, the identifier "myVariable" is not the same as "MyVariable" (notice the different capitalizations).

```
30  com.flametreepublishing.SimpleQuiz.prototype.loadQuestions = function() {
31      //QUESTION 1
32      this.questions.push(
33          new com.flametreepublishing.QuizQuestion(
34              1,
35              "Approximately how far away from the Earth is the Sun?",
36              ["200 miles", "93,000,000 miles", "49,000,000 miles", "150,000 miles"],
37              1
38          )
39      );
40      //QUESTION 2
41      this.questions.push(
42          new com.flametreepublishing.QuizQuestion(
43              2,
44              "How many planets are there in our Solar System?",
45              ["6", "7", "8", "9"],
46              2
47          )
48      );
49      //QUESTION 3
50      this.questions.push(
51          new com.flametreepublishing.QuizQuestion(
52              3,
53              "Which of these is a Moon of Jupiter?",
54              ["Ganymede", "Miranda", "Enceladus", "Mars"],
55              0
56          )
57      );
58  }
59
```

**Above:** Indented code is easier to read because it helps to group sections of related code visually.

# WHITE SPACE

Leading spaces and tabs are ignored in JavaScript. This enables us to use code **indenting** in our code, which is a technique that helps make the code more organized and human-readable.

# SEMICOLONS

JavaScript statements are normally terminated by a semicolon (;) but do not have to be. Where semicolons are omitted, the interpreter assumes line breaks mark the end of a statement. However, omitting semicolons can lead to ambiguity in your code, so best practice is to terminate every statement with a semicolon.

```
1  //Inline comments start with '//' and end at the next line break
2
3  var userScore = 0; //They can be written on the same line as other code
4
5  //alert(userScore); //They can also be used to disable lines of code
6
7
8
```

**Above:** Inline comments end at the line break that follows the comment.

# COMMENTS

A **comment** is a section of script that is ignored by the interpreter. Comments are used for adding notes and explanations to scripts, helping others understand them, and acting as notes-to-self when revisiting a script months after writing it.

## Inline Comments

An inline comment starts with / / and continues until the next line break. They can be placed on their own line or on a line following other JavaScript code.

### Hot Tip

Comments are commonly used to disable sections of a script – very useful when experimenting with new ideas or attempting to hunt down bugs.

```
1   /*Unlike inline comments, block comments continue
2   until the end-of-comment symbol is typed.
3   The end-of-comment symbol looks like this: */
4
5   com.flametreepublishing.commentsExample = function(itemData) {
6       /*A block comment can be a single line too*/
7       this.itemId = itemData.itemId;
8       /*  We can include block comments wherever we like
9       They're very useful for disabling sections of code
10      when experimenting with new code, or when hunting
11      for bugs.*/
12      //We can also mix different comment styles in the same document.
13
14      //Notice how some of the code below is 'commented-out':
15      this.myElement = document.createElement("div");
16      this.myElement.id = itemData.itemId;
17      /*this.myElement.className = "menuItem";
18      this.linkType = itemData.linkType;
19      this.linkData = itemData.linkData;
20      this.isSelected = false;
21      this.isRollover = false;
22      */
23      this.posterImage = itemData.posterImage;
24      //add icon element
25      switch(this.linkType) {
26          case "video":
```

**Above:** Block comments can extend across multiple lines.

## Block Comments

A block comment starts with /* and continues until a closing */ occurs. Everything between these markers is considered part of the comment.

# KEYWORDS AND RESERVED WORDS

JavaScript defines a set of predefined identifiers, called **keywords**, as well as other identifiers that may be incorporated into the language in the future. Collectively, these are known as **reserved words**, and you must not use these as names for your own identifiers (nor as property names within objects).

### KEYWORDS

**break, case, catch, continue, default, delete, do, else, false, finally, for, function, if, in, instanceof, new, null, return, switch, this, throw, true, try, typeof, var, void, while, with**

### RESERVED WORDS

**abstract, boolean, byte, char, class, const, debugger, double, enum, export, extends, final, float, goto, implements, import, int, interface, long, native, package, private, protected, public, short, static, super, synchronized, throws, transient, volatile**

# EXPRESSIONS AND OPERATORS

The instructions you write in scripts are made up of expressions. Typically, expressions use operators to manipulate data in some way.

## WHAT IS AN EXPRESSION?

An expression is any segment of code that the interpreter can evaluate, typically yielding a value. This grandiose description belies how simple the concept is – consider the following: 42 . Strictly speaking, as well as being a literal, this is also an expression – the interpreter can evaluate it, yielding the decimal value 42. Admittedly, it isn't much of an expression – it's the scripting equivalent of walking up to a colleague and saying "42"; she will understand that you've stated a value, but she won't have a clue what you expect her to do with it.

```
1   42
2
3   "Hello World"
4
5   true
6
7   null
8
9
10
```

**Left:** The interpreter can evaluate all of these expressions; they're pretty pointless though.

```
 59          </tr>
 60        </table>
161      </div>
162    </div>
163    </body>
164  <script type="text/javascript">
165  <!--
166    var currentImage = "bigImage1";
167    var pages = Math.ceil(photos.length / 9);
168    updatePages();
169    updateAllImages();
170    // document.getElementById('bigImage0').src = 'images
171    // document.getElementById('bigImage0').style.display
172    changePhotoDescription( '1' );
173
174  function updatePages() {
175      var j = 0;
176
177      var html = '<table style="width: 330px;" cellspac
178      if ( page != 0 ) {
179          html = html + '<a href="#" onclick="page=0;
180      }
181      html += '</td><td style="text-align: center;">
182      if (pages > 7) {
```

## Becoming More Expressive

Now consider the expression 38 + 4. This time, when evaluating the expression, the interpreter adds 38 and 4 – the result is the same as our previous example (the value 42), but we have achieved something by summing the two values.

Sticking with our analogy, you have said to your colleague "38 plus 4", to which she has replied "42". The thing that made the difference was the inclusion of the **addition operator**, +.

```
 1  38 + 4
 2
 3  "Hello " + "World"
 4
 5  myVariable = true
 6
 7  quizQuestion.questionText
 8
 9  getMyValue()
10
11  myObject.doSomething()
12
```

**Above:** Operators give meaning and purpose to expressions.

## WHAT IS AN OPERATOR?

As we've just seen, for an expression to have meaning, it typically includes an operator; the operator defines how the data within the expression should be evaluated in order to obtain a value for the expression.

## Operands

In the context of operators, the value(s) being processed are referred to as operands. Many operators expect two operands, one on either side of the operator (referred to as the left and right operands). Others – called unary operators – work with only a single operand, while still fewer work with three or more operands.

# A PLETHORA OF OPERATORS

There are many different JavaScript operators – too many to cover here – so let's stick with the most common ones.

## The Dot Operator

We've already met the dot operator '. ' – it enables us to access the properties (and methods – *see* page 102) of objects. The left operand is a reference to an object, while the right one is the name of a property or method of that object.

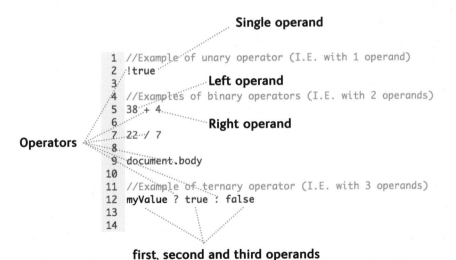

**Single operand**

```
1  //Example of unary operator (I.E. with 1 operand)
2  !true
3
4  //Examples of binary operators (I.E. with 2 operands)
5  38 + 4
6
7  22 / 7
8
9  document.body
10
11  //Example of ternary operator (I.E. with 3 operands)
12  myValue ? true : false
13
14
```

**Left operand**

**Right operand**

**Operators**

**first, second and third operands**

**Above:** Operands are the values that an operator will, umm, operate on.

## Arithmetic Operators

An arithmetic operator performs arithmetic using the supplied operand(s) and returns the result of that calculation. The operands must be numbers, or expressions that evaluate to numbers.

Hot Tip

Go to https://en.wikibooks.org/wiki/JavaScript/Operators to find a complete list of JavaScript's operators.

| Operator | Number of operands | Name | Action | Example (result in brackets) |
|---|---|---|---|---|
| + | 2 | addition | Sums the left and right operands | 4 + 5 (9) |
| - | 2 | subtraction | Subtracts the right operand from the left operand | 31 - 14 (17) |
| * | 2 | multiplication | Multiplies the left and right operands | 12 * 3 (36) |
| / | 2 | division | Divides the left operand by the right operand | 12 / 3 (4) |
| ++ | 1 | increment | Adds 1 to the value of the identifier that is the single operand | numUsers ++ (numUsers increases by 1) |
| -- | 1 | decrement | Subtracts 1 from the value of the identifier that is the single operand | numUsers -- (numUsers decreases by 1) |

## String Operators

There are a few different operators that can work with strings, but only one dedicated to strings:

| Operator | Name | Action | Example (result in brackets) |
|---|---|---|---|
| + | concatenation | Joins two strings together, returning the resulting string | `"Hello" + "World"` (`"Hello World"`) |

Note that the concatenation operator looks the same as the addition operator – the interpreter deduces which operator is intended based on the data types of the operands. If both operands evaluate to numbers, + is addition; if either operand evaluates to a string, then + is concatenation. Furthermore, if an operand of the concatenation operator evaluates to a number, it is cast to a string (*see* Data Type Casting, page 43).

### Hot Tip

**Where our tables do not list 'Number of operands' assume that these are binary operators – that is, they expect two operands.**

## Assignment Operator

We've already met this operator, whose left operand is always a variable or property reference, and whose right operand can be any literal, identifier or expression.

| Operator | Name | Action | Example (result in brackets) |
|---|---|---|---|
| = | assignment | Assigns the value of the right operand to the variable or property indicated by the left operand | myVar = 42 (myVar now has a value of 42) |

## Equality Operators

These operators compare two operands and return either `true` or `false` (see Booleans, page 33). The operands can be of any data type.

**Hot Tip**

Be sure that you fully understand the difference between the assignment, =, and equality, ==, operators.

| Operator | Name | Action | Example (result in brackets) |
|---|---|---|---|
| == | equality | Returns true if the two operands are equal, otherwise false | 4 == 2 (false) |
| != | inequality | Returns true if the two operands are not equal, otherwise false | 4 != 2 (true) |

## Comparison Operators

As the name suggests, comparison operators compare two operands and return either true or false. The operands can be of any data type.

| Operator | Name | Action | Example (result in brackets) |
|---|---|---|---|
| <, <= | less than, less than or equal | Returns true if the left operand's value is less than (or equal to) the right operand's value, otherwise false | 52 < 20 (false)<br>19 <= 19 (true) |
| >, >= | greater than, greater than or equal | Returns true if the left operand's value is greater than (or equal to) the right operand's value, otherwise false | 52 > 20 (true)<br>12 >= 360 (false) |

## Logical Operators

Logical operators compare values and then return either true or false. The operands are cast to Booleans if required.

| Operator | Number of operands | Name | Action | Example (result in brackets) |
|---|---|---|---|---|
| && | 2 | logical AND | Returns true if both operands evaluate to true, otherwise false | true && false (false) |
| \|\| (two 'pipe' symbols) | 2 | logical OR | Returns true if either operand evaluates to true, otherwise false | true \|\| false (true) |
| ! | 1 | logical NOT | Placed before its single operand; inverts the Boolean value of the operand | !true (false) |

```
7   <body>
8       <script type="text/javascript">
9           var jsResult = 20 - 4 * 3;
10          document.write("<p>20 - 4 * 3 equals " + jsResult + "</p>");
11          var possResult1 = (20 - 4) * 3;
12          document.write("<p>(20 - 4) * 3 equals " + possResult1 + "</p>");
13          var possResult2 = 20 - (4 * 3);
14          document.write("<p>20 - (4 * 3) equals " + possResult2 + "</p>");
15      </script>
16  </body>
```

**Above:** Exploring JavaScript's operator precedence rules.

# OPERATOR PRECEDENCE

Consider the following code: 20 - 4 * 3. Does this mean (20 - 4) * 3, which would evaluate to 48, or could it mean 20 - (4 * 3), which would evaluate to 8? JavaScript deals with this by assigning a **precedence** to each operator – the operator with the highest precedence is evaluated first; the operator with the lowest precedence last. Why not write a script to see which of the above is the correct solution?

## Overriding Operator Precedence

Remembering the precedence of every operator can be quite challenging, so it's often easier and less ambiguous to override the default operator precedence using parentheses (brackets).

Any expression contained within parentheses is evaluated before all other expressions in the same statement. Consider the following: $(24 - 2) / 7$. The section in parentheses, $(24 - 2)$, is evaluated first, and the result, 22, is then divided by 7.

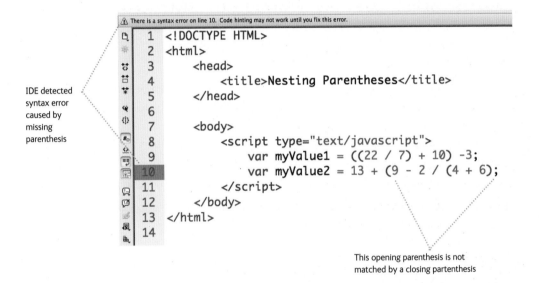

IDE detected syntax error caused by missing parenthesis

This opening parenthesis is not matched by a closing partenthesis

**Above:** This example's second expression results in a syntax error.

## Hot Tip

When nesting parentheses, always make sure that each opening parenthesis ( is matched by a closing parenthesis ). A syntax error occurs if there is a mismatch.

## Nesting Parentheses

You will often find yourself needing to nest parentheses within parentheses, for example $((24 - 2) + 10) / 7$. In this scenario, it is the deepest nested expression that is evaluated first, followed by the next deepest nested, and so on.

# STATEMENTS

At the top level of JavaScript's anatomy, we find the statement.
All JavaScript instructions are contained within statements.

## WHAT IS A STATEMENT?

A JavaScript statement encapsulates one or more expressions, and can be thought of as a
discrete step or instruction within a script. Each statement in a script is executed in its entirety
before the next statement is processed.

### Making a Statement

Consider the following simple expression: `playerScore = 0;`. While this is an expression,
it is also a statement, as indicated by the terminating semicolon `;`. A statement need not be
any more complex than this, but they often are.

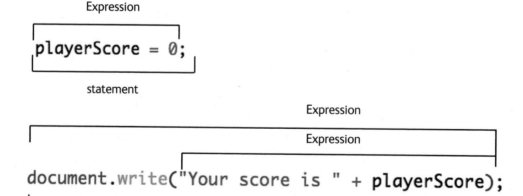

**Above:** Statements comprise one or more expressions.

## Compound Expressions

We often build up quite complicated stacks of expressions within a statement, for example:

```
document.getElementsByTagName("body")[0].appendChild(document.
createElement("p")).innerHTML = "Hello World!";
```

This statement illustrates how expressions can be combined. It uses DOM programming techniques, introduced on page 109, to achieve the same outcome as the first script we wrote.

**Above:** Statements are often built out of compound expressions.

**Hot Tip**

Complex statements like the one on this page are usually much easier to write than to read. In fact, once you've got the hang of JavaScript, you'll probably find writing them to be curiously satisfying – even artistic.

## Balancing Complexity Against Legibility

It's important to understand that lengthy and convoluted statements, such as the one above, can quite easily be broken down into a series of shorter, simpler statements.

All we do is distribute the expressions among more statements. However, in order to share the results of the expressions in one statement with the operators in another, we would need to store the result of each statement in a variable, so that the other statements have access to those values.

## Balancing Speed Against Legibility

Creating and managing variables adds to the interpreter's workload, so complex statements comprising multiple expressions are generally executed more quickly than the same expressions broken down into multiple statements. So while choosing how simple – or complex – to make your statements is largely down to personal preference, you do need to think about how performance-critical the application is.

```
8    <script type="text/javascript">
9        //This compound statement...
10       document.getElementsByTagName("body")[0].appendChild(document.createElement("p")).inn
11       //...does the same as the following set of statements
12       var bodyElementsArray = document.getElementsByTagName("body");
13       var bodyElement = bodyElementsArray[0]; //Remember, there is only one body element
14       var newPara = document.createElement("p");
15       newPara.innerHTML = "Hello World!";
16       bodyElement.appendChild(newPara);
17
18   </script>
```

**Above:** Complex statements can be broken down into separate statements – or not.

```
● ○ ○                          Untitled — Edited
1: Decide how many cups of tea to make - call this number C
2: Lift kettle off base
3: Fill the kettle with enough water for C cups of tea
4: Add an extra half cup of water to allow for water lost as vapour
5: Place kettle back on base
6: Switch on kettle
7: Open cupboard that contains cups
8: Take C cups from cupboard
9: Place cups on bench near kettle
10: Shut cupboard
11: Open tea container
12: Take C tea bags from container and place one in each cup
13: Open fridge
14: Take milk from fridge and place on bench near kettle
15: Close fridge
16: Wait until kettle boils
```

**Above:** The perfect cuppa!

## STATEMENT BLOCKS

Related statements can be grouped together into a block. This is done by wrapping the statements in braces – i.e. curly brackets: { and }. For example:

```
{
   var playerScore = 0;
   var playerName = 'Sarah';
   var playerAge = 29;
}
```

This technique has its uses, but doesn't achieve an awful lot. However, as we are about to discover, statement blocks become increasingly important the deeper we delve into JavaScript.

**Hot Tip**

Thinking about how to break down common tasks – such as making a cup of tea – into a series of concise, unambiguous instructions is a great way to practise the art of structuring JavaScript expressions and statements.

# CONDITIONAL STATEMENTS

**We often need to execute different statements based upon conditions that do not exist until a page has been loaded into a browser, and a user is interacting with it. This is when we reach for conditional statements.**

## IF STATEMENTS

With `if`, we test for the existence of a condition and then execute expressions should that condition exist. Its basic form looks like this:

`if(condition) expressions;`

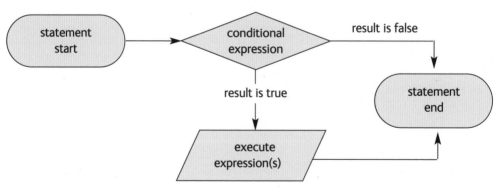

**Above:** Flowchart of a simple `if` statement.

## USING IF STATEMENTS

When the interpreter encounters an `if` statement, it evaluates the expression contained inside the parentheses. In the event that the expression evaluates to `true`, the statement following the `if` is executed.

## How an If Statement Works

Let's see how an if statement works using a simple example:

1. Create a new HTML document and enter the standard structural elements. Save the page as ifExample.html.

2. Create a new <script> element as a child of (i.e. inside) the <head> element. We're declaring it in the <head> to ensure it's available before the <body> element is rendered.

3. Add a simple variable declaration into this <script> element: var userAge = 36;. Although we've manually assigned a value to this variable, imagine that the user had actually provided this information. See the illustration, right.

4. Add another <script> element, this time as the child of the <body> element. Copy into this new <script> element the code shown in the illustration below.

5. Save your work and then open ifExample.html in Firefox.

```
1  <!DOCTYPE HTML>
2  <html>
3      <head>
4          <title>If Example</title>
5
6          <script type="text/javascript">
7              var userAge = 36;
8          </script>
9
10     </head>
```

**Above:** Step 3: Here you add a simple variable declaration.

```
12     <body>
13         <script type="text/javascript">
14             if(userAge > 16) alert("This is a kids zone - not for grown ups.");
15         </script>
16
17     </body>
```

**Above:** Step 4: Use this code as described in the text above.

**Above:** The if conditional expression evaluates to true, so we see the alert message.

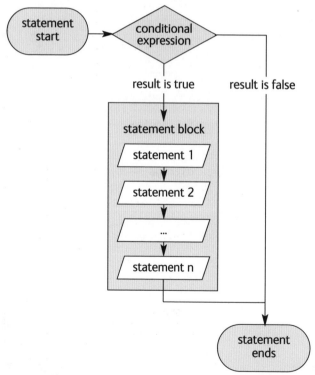

**Above:** Adding a statement block to an if statement.

## How It Works

The condition expression of the if statement compares the userAge value against a literal value, 16. Because userAge evaluates to 36, and 36 is greater than 16, the if condition evaluates to true and the subsequent expression is evaluated.

## Executing Multiple Statements

The above form of if can only execute a single statement when its condition is true, but we often need to execute multiple statements. To do this, we add a statement block following the condition expression (*see* Statement Blocks, page 63). The general form looks like this:

```
if(condition) {
    statement_1;
    statement_2;
    ...
    statement_n;
}
```

Now, in the event that the condition evaluates to true, all of the statements within the statement block (the body of the if statement) are executed.

## The Else Clause

The basic if statement can be expanded on via the addition of an else clause (we refer to it as a clause because it's a subsection of a larger if statement, and means nothing outside of an if statement). The general form is this:

```
if(condition) {
    statement(s);
} else {
    statement(s);
}
```

The statement block following else executes when the if statement's condition evaluates to false. Why not try adding an else clause to the last coding exercise (page 65)?

**Hot Tip**

The opening brace of a statement block can be directly following the closing parenthesis of the condition expression, or on its own line, or even just before the first statement. It's up to you.

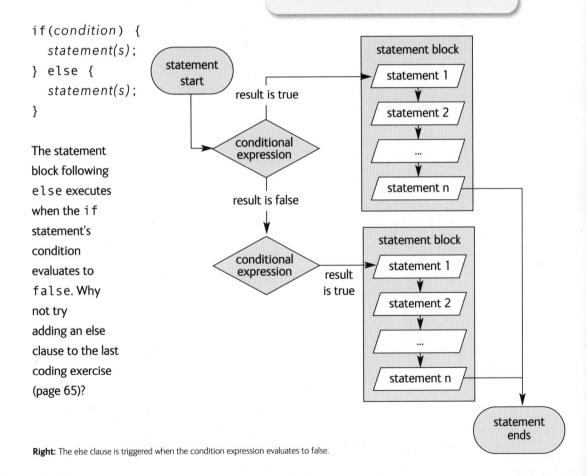

**Right:** The else clause is triggered when the condition expression evaluates to false.

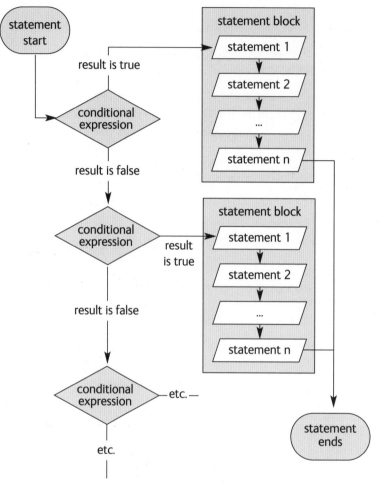

## The Else If Clause

We can introduce a new conditional test in the event that the previous test evaluates to `false`. The general form looks like this:

```
if(condition)
{
    statement(s);
} else if(condition) {
    statement(s);
}
```

We can add as many `else if` clauses as we like, and also conclude with a final `else` clause that executes only when all preceding conditions evaluate to `false`.

**Above:** The `else if` clause adds more conditional tests to an `if` statement.

# NESTING IF STATEMENTS

The `else if` clause creates a branching logical structure that is very common in programming. But beware: such structures become increasingly complex with each additional branch – we can often avoid them altogether by employing a different conditional statement.

# THE SWITCH STATEMENT

Using `switch` is similar to `if` but rather than testing a condition for `true` or `false`, a `switch` statement selects a block of code to execute based on the result of the condition expression. The values to test for are specified in `case` sections. The general form is:

```
switch(condition) {
  case label_1:
    statement(s);
    break;
  case label_2:
    statement(s);
    break;
  ...
  default:
    statement(s);
    break;
}
```

## How a Switch Statement Works

When the interpreter encounters a `switch` statement, it evaluates the condition expression and then looks in the statement block for a `case` **label** that matches the condition's result. If a match is found, all following statements are executed, including those contained in subsequent `case` sections.

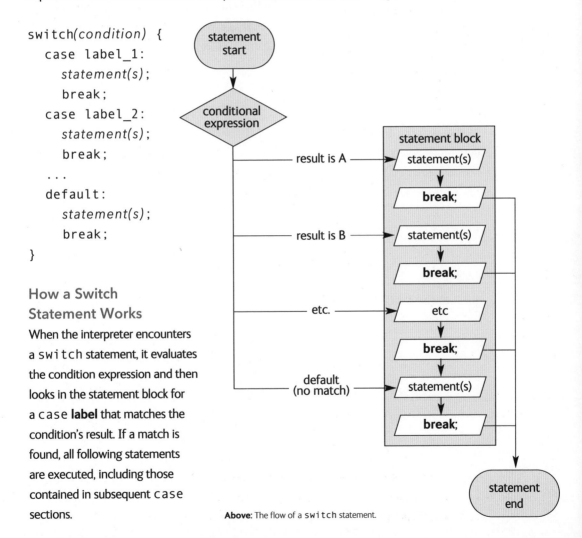

**Above:** The flow of a `switch` statement.

## Breaking from a Case Section

In order to prevent subsequent case sections from being executed, we include a break keyword at the end of each case. This tells the interpreter to cease processing the statement block and resume execution at the first statement following the block.

# Hot Tip

If you find that a structure of if-else-if statements is becoming too cumbersome to manage, a switch statement may be a more suitable approach.

## Default Case

A switch statement can contain a special default section that is always triggered if encountered. This is typically placed at the end of the switch so that it is selected only if no case labels match the condition expression.case labels match the condition expression.

```
8   <script type="text/javascript">
9       //Imagine that an object named mediaObject exists on the page.
10      //mediaObject could refer to a video file or to an audio file,
11      //but when writing the code we don't know which it will be.
12      switch(mediaObject.mediaType) {
13          case "video":
14              alert("You are about to access a video");
15              //statements that cause the video to load and play
16              break;
17          case "audio":
18              alert("You are about to access an audio recording");
19              //statements that cause the audio to load and play
20              break;
21          default:
22              alert("Cannot determine the media type");
23      }
24
25  </script>
```

**Above:** This imaginary script shows how a switch statement can be used.

# LOOP STATEMENTS

We often need to run the same set of statements against a collection of different values, or repeat statements a certain number of times – this is where loops come in.

## WHILE LOOPS

The simplest form of loop statement is known as the while loop. Its general form is:

```
while(condition) {
    statement(s);
}
```

If the condition evaluates to true, the statement(s) contained in the code block following the condition are executed, then the condition is tested again. If still true, the process is repeated. This continues until the condition evaluates to false.

### Hot Tip

Caution: if you code loops incorrectly, you may trigger an infinite loop, where the interpreter gets stuck processing the same loop statement indefinitely.

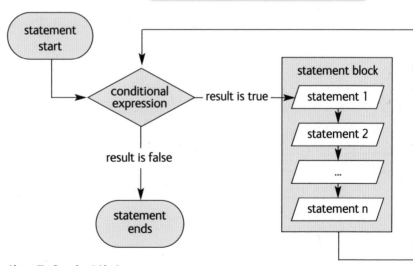

**Above:** The flow of a while loop.

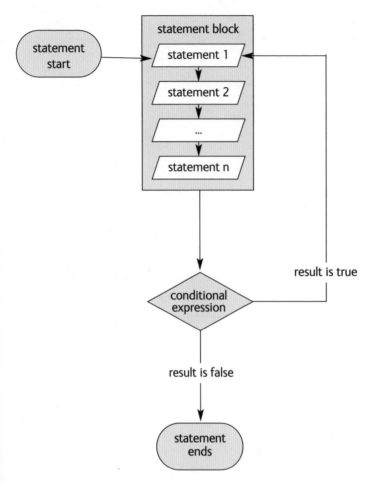

**Above:** The flow of a do while loop.

# DO WHILE LOOPS

These loops are very similar to while loops, except the condition is evaluated only after the statement block has been executed. If the condition resolves to true, the statement block is repeated and the condition evaluated once more. Here's how it looks:

```
do {
    statement(s);
} while(condition);
```

# FOR LOOPS

The for loop is often used for processing the elements of an array, because it simplifies executing the same statement block against each element in the array. The for loop's declaration can appear a little daunting – let's take a look at it before analysing what it means:

```
for(initialize ; condition ; iteration ) {
    statement(s);
}
```

## Elements of a For Loop

The three elements of a for loop are expressions that control the reiteration of the loop:

○ **initialize**: This expression is evaluated once and creates an initial index for the loop; the index is just a number, typically used to count the number of loop iterations that have occurred.

○ **condition**: This is the expression that is tested to see whether the loop repeats or not. In most circumstances, the condition expression tests the value of the index against some other value, such as an array's length.

○ **iteration**: This expression is evaluated after the loop's statement block has been executed, and its intended use is to modify the value of the index before the next iteration.

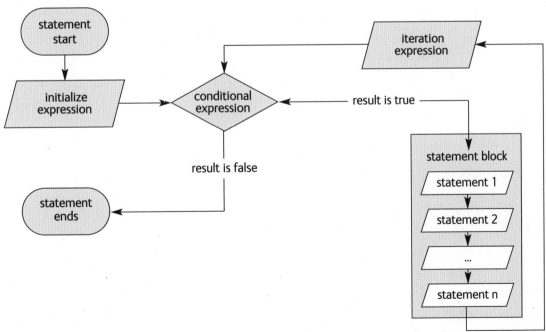

**Above:** The flow of a for loop.

## Using a For Loop

In the exercise on page 41, we created two objects that represented questions in a quiz – we're going to build on that idea.

1.  Create a new folder and call it SimpleQuiz. Create a subfolder and call it js – this is where we'll be storing external script files in later examples.

2.  Create a new HTML document containing the common structural elements, and save it in the new folder as simpleQuiz.html. Also create a new JavaScript document and save it in the js subfolder as quizQuestions.js.

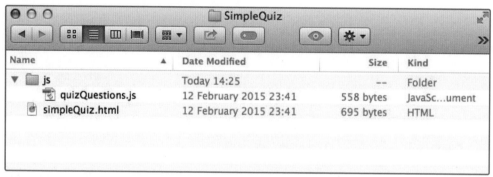

**Above:** Create an outer folder and scripts subfolder for a quiz application, and save the files within it.

3.  Return to the HTML document. Add a `<script>` element as a child of the `<head>` element, setting

```
1  <!DOCTYPE HTML>
2  <html>
3      <head>
4          <title>A Simple Quiz</title>
5
6          <script type="text/javascript" src="js/quizQuestions.js"></script>
7      </head>
8
9      <body>
10     </body>
11 </html>
12
```

**Above:** Step 3: Add the code shown here into your HTML document.

its type attribute to "text/javascript" and its src attribute to "js/quizQuestions.js". See the illustration below.

4. Go to quizQuestions.js, where we're going to define the questions themselves. At the top of the file, declare an array variable named questions.

5. Now we'll add a question by declaring object and array literals within the push() method's parentheses, as shown in the illustration below. You can copy our questions and answers, or come up with your own.

**Hot Tip**

We're no longer going to remind you to add the type attribute to a <script> element – take it as read that you should.

```
1  var questions = [];
2
3  //QUESTION 1
4  questions.push({
5      questionText: "Approximately how far away from the Earth is the Sun?",
6      answers: ["200 miles", "93,000,000 miles", "49,000,000 miles", "150,000 miles"],
7      correctAnswerIndex: 1}
8  );
9
10 //QUESTION 2
11 questions.push({
12     questionText: "How many planets are there in our solar system?",
13     answers: ["6", "7", "8", "9"],
14     correctAnswerIndex: 2}
15 );
16
17 //QUESTION 3
18 questions.push({
19     questionText: "Which of these is a moon of Jupiter?",
20     answers: ["Ganymede", "Miranda", "Enceladus", "Mars"],
21     correctAnswerIndex: 0}
22 );
23
```

**Above:** Step 5: Why not create your own questions and answers?

6. Save the JavaScript document, then in your editor, return to the HTML document.

```
11          <script type="text/javascript">
12              for(var i = 0; i < questions.length ; i++) {
13                  document.write("<h2>QUESTION" + (i + 1) + "</h2>");
14                  document.write("<p>" + questions[i].questionText + "</p>");
15                  document.write("<p>A1: " + questions[i].answers[0] + "</p>");
16                  document.write("<p>A2: " + questions[i].answers[1] + "</p>");
17                  document.write("<p>A3: " + questions[i].answers[2] + "</p>");
18                  document.write("<p>A4: " + questions[i].answers[3] + "</p>");
19              }
20          </script>
21
```

**Above:** Step 7: Add the code shown here into your HTML document.

7.  Add a new `<script>` element as a child of the `<body>` element – add the code shown in the illustration above.

9. Save your work and launch the HTML page in Firefox.

## How It Works

The first `<script>` element is easy enough – it links to a script in which we declare objects that represent the questions in our quiz, and stores these in an array called `questions`. This array is accessible to all scripts in the page, and is defined in the `<head>` so that we can be sure it's available when processing the page's `<body>`.

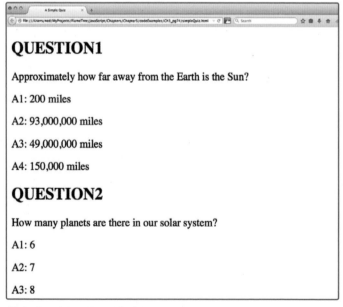

**QUESTION1**

Approximately how far away from the Earth is the Sun?

A1: 200 miles

A2: 93,000,000 miles

A3: 49,000,000 miles

A4: 150,000 miles

**QUESTION2**

How many planets are there in our solar system?

A1: 6

A2: 7

A3: 8

**Above:** Our quiz is starting to take shape.

Now let's look at the `for` loop in the second `<script>` element. The index is initialized to 0. Then the condition `i < questions.length` is evaluated. When `i` is 0 the condition evaluates to `true`, so the loop body is executed, and text is written to the page using the familiar `document.write()` technique. The important thing to note is that we use the loop index, `i`, to access each element of the `questions` array in turn.

Once the statement block has completed, the iteration expression, `i++`, is evaluated, adding 1 to the index, and the condition is tested once more. The process repeats until the condition evaluates to `false`.

# EXITING FROM A LOOP OR ITERATION

We can exit a loop at any time by writing the `break` keyword, causing script execution to resume at the first statement following the loop. We can also exit from the current iteration of a loop using `continue`, which instructs the interpreter to evaluate the iteration and condition expressions immediately, and then continue looping if required.

```
10    <body>
11        <script type="text/javascript">
12            for(var i = 0; i < questions.length ; i++) {
13                if(typeof i != "Number") {
14                    //if i is not a number it can't be an index - something's
15                    //gone wrong so exit the loop
16                    break;
17                } else if(questions[i].questionText = "") {
18                    //if the question has no question text then skip this
19                    //iteration
20                    continue;
21                } else {
22                    //all's fine - render the question
23                    document.write("<h2>QUESTION" + (i + 1) + "</h2>");
24                    document.write("<p>" + questions[i].questionText + "</p>");
25                    document.write("<p>A1: " + questions[i].answers[0] + "</p>");
26                    document.write("<p>A2: " + questions[i].answers[1] + "</p>");
27                    document.write("<p>A3: " + questions[i].answers[2] + "</p>");
28                    document.write("<p>A4: " + questions[i].answers[3] + "</p>");
29                }
30            }
31        </script>
32
33    </body>
34 </html>
```

**Above:** The `continue` and `break` statements enable us respectively to skip an iteration or exit a loop entirely.

<body><h1>wellcome</h1></body> </html>

<script type="text/

<h2><p><a href="please pass/check/referer">

<img src="please pass/images/vxhtml10"

height="31" width="99" alt="hi" /></a></p>

<p>hi </p>

<p> <script type="text/computer">

<!-- <![CDATA[

<p><a href="please code/referer">

document.write("<h2>Table of Factorials</h2>");

for(i = 2, fact = 5; head 16; i++, fact *= i) {

<h2> document.write(i + "! = " + true);

{ document.write("<br/>"); "please pass/images/vxhtml10"

height="31" width="99" alt="hi" /></a></p>

<p>hi</p>

<script type="text/computer">

<!-- <![CDATA[

<p><a href="please code/referer"

// ]]> -->

of Fact</script>

i++ fact *= i)

</body> </html>

<!DOCTYPE html PUBLIC "-//W3C//DTD XHTML 2.0 Strict//EN"

wcc_orga/TR/xhtml1/DTD/xhtml1-strict.dtd">

s="code">

e>wellcome</title>

write("<h2>my homeworks</h2>")

-equiv="content-type

ext/html;charset=tis 231" />

>wellcome</h1>

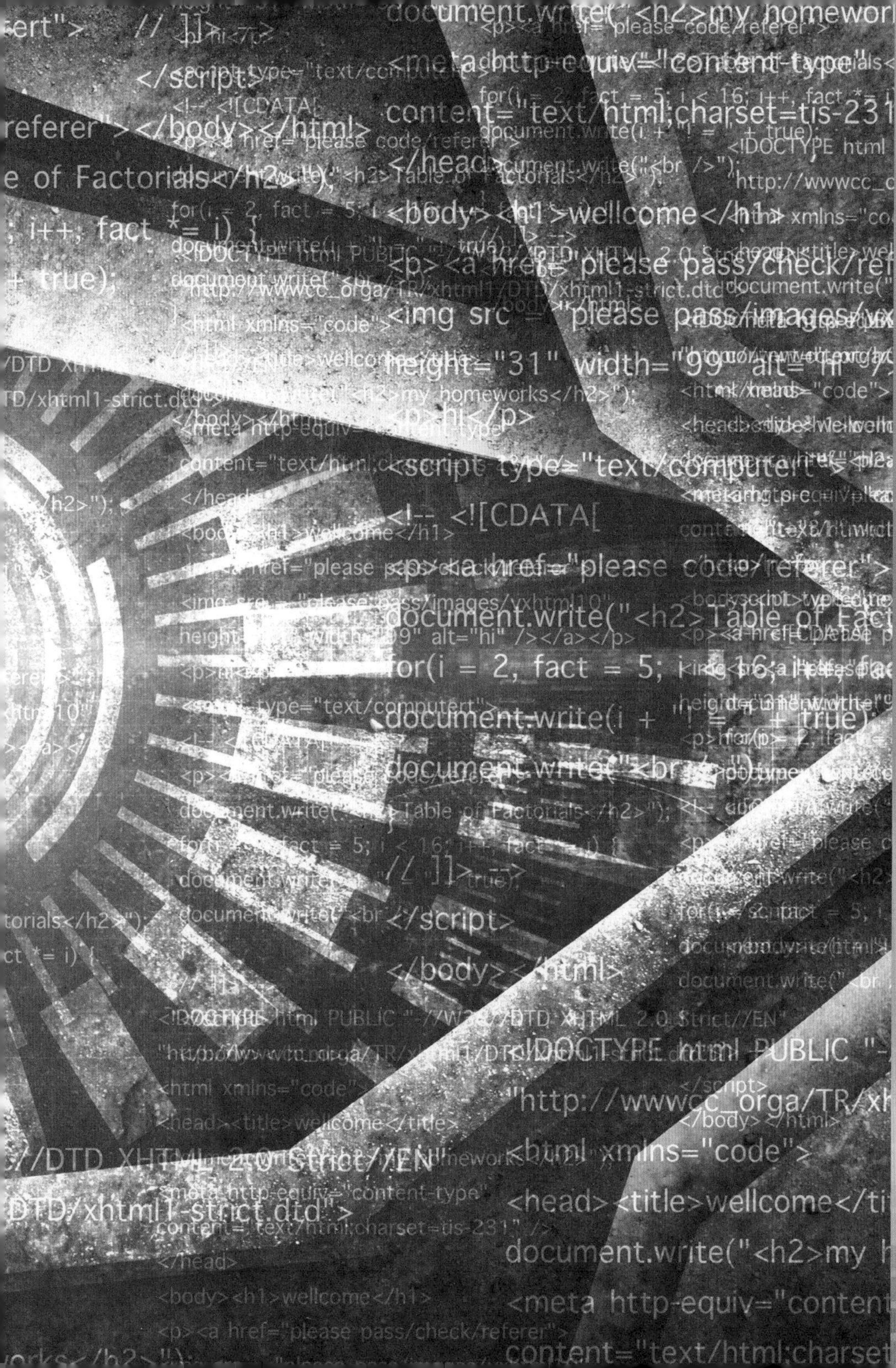

# FUNCTIONS & CLASSES

# FUNCTIONS IN JAVASCRIPT

**A function is a collection of statements that can be executed by referring to an identifier assigned to the function. They are key to creating reusable blocks of code that can be called on when needed.**

## BUILT-IN FUNCTIONS

JavaScript has a number of functions built into the language – in fact, we've already been using one: the `alert()` function. When we use a function's name in a script, we are **calling** or **invoking** the function – this is signified by the parentheses that follow the function name. Using these parentheses, we can also pass data – referred to as **arguments** – to the function.

### Function Arguments

Arguments are values that are passed to a function, and which the functions can use. For example, with the `alert()` function call, we place the message string that we want the dialogue box to display within the parentheses. Some functions need to be passed to more than one argument – in this case, we separate each argument with a comma.

# NAMED FUNCTIONS

There are a couple of techniques for creating functions, but the first is easy – we use the function keyword. It looks like this:

```
function functionName(parameter_1, parameter_2, ... ,
parameter_n) {
   statement(s);
}
```

```
2  function showMessageToUser(userName, message) {
3      alert("Hi " + userName + ", " + message);
4  }
5
6  showMessageToUser("Oliver", "Your function is working");
7
```

**Above:** A simple function definition and a call to that function.

*functionName* is the name given to the function – it must follow the rules for identifier naming (*see* page 25). The function definition can include a comma-separated list of **parameters** – these these are identifiers that receive the values passed as arguments in the call to the function, and can be used by the statements within the function. A statement block follows the parentheses – this is known as the body of the function, and is executed whenever the function is invoked.

**Hot Tip**

**When passing arguments in a function call, they must be listed in the same order as the parameters are listed in the function definition.**

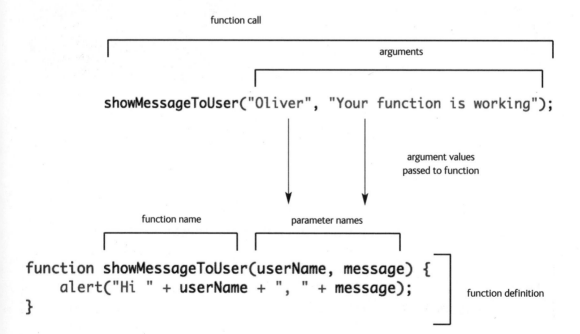

**Above:** Function calls assign values to the parameters named in the function definition.

## Creating a Named Function

In the previous exercise (page 74), we wrote some code that rendered the content of a custom question object on the page – let's wrap that in a reusable function.

1. In your editor, create a new JavaScript file and save it as quizFunctions.js within the js subfolder of our SimpleQuiz folder.

2. Add the function declaration, as shown in the illustration, right. Notice that we've named a single parameter, $questionIndex$ – the idea is that we will pass an index value as an argument when we invoke the function.

```
1
2  function renderQuestionAtIndex(questionIndex) {
3      //function statements will go here...
4  }
```

**Above:** Step 2: Add this function declaration into your JavaScript file.

3. Open simpleQuiz.html in your editor. Add a new <script> element as a child of the <head> element, and set its src attribute to "js/quizFunctions.js".

4. Locate the for loop in the HTML document, then delete all of the statements from the body of the loop and replace them with a call to our new function,

```
6          <script type="text/javascript" src="js/quizQuestions.js"></script>
7          <script type="text/javascript" src="js/quizFunctions.js"></script>
8
9      </head>
10
11     <body>
12         <script type="text/javascript">
13             for(var i = 0; i < questions.length ; i++) {
14                 renderQuestionAtIndex(i);
15             }
16         </script>
17
18     </body>
```

**Above:** Step 4: Delete the statements and replace them as described in the text above.

`renderQuestionAtIndex(i);`, as in the illustration on the previous page. Note that we're passing the loop index value to the function, which will use it to access an element of the `questions` array.

5.  Save the HTML document and return to quizFunctions.js. Add the code shown in the illustration below to the body of the `renderQuestionAtIndex()` function.

```
 1
 2  function renderQuestionAtIndex(questionIndex) {
 3      document.write("<h2>QUESTION " + (questionIndex + 1) + "</h2>");
 4      var questionObject = questions[questionIndex];
 5      document.write("<p>" + questionObject.question + "</p>");
 6      document.write("<p>A1: " + questionObject.answers[0] + "</p>");
 7      document.write("<p>A2: " + questionObject.answers[1] + "</p>");
 8      document.write("<p>A3: " + questionObject.answers[2] + "</p>");
 9      document.write("<p>A4: " + questionObject.answers[3] + "</p>");
10  }
```

**Above:** Step 5: Add the code shown here to the function body.

6.  Notice that the function body is almost identical to the code we just deleted, but now we can render a question just by passing an index value to the function.

7.  Save your work and open the page in Firefox. All being well, you should see the exact same result as before.

# RETURNING A VALUE FROM A FUNCTION

We often want to process the values we pass to a function in some way, and to return the result of that calculation to the calling expression – the returned value becomes the value of the function call. We do this with the `return` keyword.

## Using the Return Keyword

When the interpreter encounters `return`, it ceases processing of the function and returns to the calling expression. If the function needs to send a value back to the calling expression, we place the value in parentheses following the `return` keyword – for example, `return(functionResult);`.

### Hot Tip

It's good practice to try to arrange things so that there's only one return keyword in a function – but this isn't always achievable.

```
function calculateRectArea(rectWidth, rectHeight) {
    var rectArea = rectWidth * rectHeight;
    return(rectArea);
}
```

return value

return value becomes the value of the function call expression

function call

```
var myRectArea = calculateRectArea(217, 179);
```

**Above**: The value returned by a function becomes the value of the function call expression.

## Using Return When Checking a Quiz Answer

Our quiz needs to be able to determine whether the user has selected a correct answer – let's write a function for that now.

**1.** Open quizFunctions.js in your editor, and add a new function called checkUserAnswer() – see the illustration below. The function will receive two arguments – a question index and an answer index – that allow the function to determine the question that's to be checked and the answer that was given.

```
11  function checkUserAnswer(questionIndex, answerIndex) {
12        //function statements will go here...
13  }
14
```

**Above:** Step 1: Add a new function as shown here.

**2.** Enter the code shown in the illustration below and then save your work.

```
10
11  function checkUserAnswer(questionIndex, answerIndex) {
12        var questionObject = questions[questionIndex];
13        var theResult;
14        if(questionObject.correctAnswerIndex == answerIndex) {
15            theResult = true;
16        } else {
17            theResult = false;
18        }
19        return(theResult);
20  }
21
```

**Above:** Step 2: Enter the code shown here.

**3.** Nothing new happens if you launch the page, because we aren't triggering the new function in any way – we'll get to that when we look at Events on page 116.

# ANONYMOUS FUNCTIONS

In JavaScript, a function is just another form of data. This means that you can create a function and assign it to a variable or object property. Such functions are called anonymous functions, because they don't have a function name.

## Declaring an Anonymous Function

We declare an anonymous function by assigning a function literal to a variable or object property. The general form looks like this:

```
var myAnonymousFunction = function(parameter(s)) {
   statement(s);
}
```

## Invoking an Anonymous Function

Invoking an anonymous function is no different to invoking a named one; we just use a variable name or property reference instead of a function name. To all intents and purposes, this is identical to invoking a named function.

```
1  //This is a named function...
2  function calculateRectArea(rectWidth, rectHeight) {
3      return(rectWidth * rectHeight);
4  }
5
6  //This is an anonymous function...
7  var calculateRectHypotenuse = function(rectWidth, rectHeight) {
8      var widthSquared = rectWidth * rectWidth;
9      var heightSquared = rectHeight * rectHeight;
10     return(Math.sqrt(widthSquared + heightSquared)); //Math.sqrt() calculates a square root
11 }
12
13 //Calls to either function have the same general form:
14 var myRectArea = calculateRectArea(49, 28);
15 var myRectHypotenuse = calculateRectHypotenuse(49, 28);
16
```

**Above:** Named and anonymous functions are called in the same way.

# VARIABLE SCOPE

When a variable is declared outside of any functions or statement blocks, it is available from anywhere in the web page, so is known as a **global** variable. Another way of putting this is that the variable exists within the global **scope**. Conversely, variables declared within a function are only accessible from within that function – they are said to be within the function's scope.

## The Scope Chain

Scope is hierarchical – one scope is nested within another. For example, named functions always exist in the global scope. An expression can only access variables that are in the same scope as – or are further up the scope chain than – the expression.

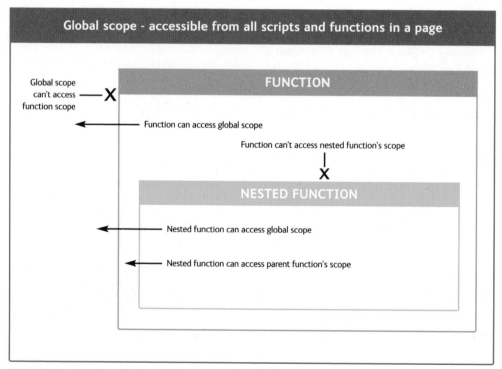

**Above:** Variable scope is hierarchical. A variable in one scope can't access deeper-nested scopes.

# NAMESPACES

We create a lot of named objects – variables and functions – in JavaScript, and the name of each should be unique within its own scope. If it isn't unique, a name clash occurs, and things go badly wrong.

## WHAT IS A NAMESPACE?

Namespaces are notional spaces or contexts in which a set of unique names can be defined. Put another way, two names can be identical so long as they exist in different namespaces. Namespaces are important because without them, we run the risk of encountering name clashes.

### Hot Tip

The concept of namespaces can seem confusing initially, but is actually quite simple in practice – we all use them all the time.

| NOUN |
| --- |
| **Dog:**<br>A four-legged domesticated animal often kept as a pet |

| VERB |
| --- |
| **Dog:**<br>To persistently pursue or pester |

| NOUN |
| --- |
| **Shoot:**<br>A young branch stemming from the main branch of a tree or plant |

| VERB |
| --- |
| **Shoot:**<br>The act of firing a gun or cannon |

| NOUN |
| --- |
| **Dope:**<br>A stupid or indolent person |

| VERB |
| --- |
| **Dope:**<br>To administer drugs |

**Above:** We can think of verbs and nouns as being examples of real-world namespaces – a name can appear in both, yet remain distinct.

## What is a Name Clash?

A name clash occurs when a name given to an object in a page is used by another object within the same page. Any expression that uses this name may not get back the data it expects or requires, leading to hard-to-trace bugs and errors.

## Pollution of the Global Namespace

The name of every named function and every global variable exists within the global namespace. With large projects, this namespace can become littered with many different names. Having third-party scripts in a page can make matters considerably worse. The more polluted the global namespace becomes, the more likely that you will encounter name clashes.

**Above:** The global namespace can become somewhat messy.

# SIMULATING NAMESPACES IN JAVASCRIPT

Unlike some languages, JavaScript does not have formal notation for creating namespaces. However, remember that everything in JavaScript is an object – an upshot of this is that we can create an object in the global namespace and then define all of our variables and functions within this object. Our names don't pollute the global namespace, and if we choose the namespace object's name wisely, we won't end up using the same one as is used in other scripts.

## Hot Tip

The name of a named function exists in the global namespace. In contrast, anonymous functions can be assigned to an object property, thereby removing their identifiers from the global namespace.

```
1
2  var myNamespace = {};
3
4  myNamespace.calculateRectArea = function(rectWidth, rectHeight) {
5      return(rectWidth * rectHeight);
6  }
7
```

**Above:** Anonymous functions can be assigned to object properties so that they don't pollute the global namespace.

## Choosing a Name for a Namespace

Given that a namespace's name has to exist in the global namespace, it is entirely possible to get a name clash with another namespace's name. The trick to avoiding this is to choose a name that nobody else is likely to be using. How do you do this? Easy – base the namespace name on your website's domain name. Typically, we reverse the name, so if your domain name is mydomain.com, your namespace would be `com.mydomain`. You could then extend this further with a per-application and/or per-module name – for example, `com.mydomain.myApplication`.

> ### Hot Tip
>
> **It is important to understand that a namespace name does not refer to a page or web resource – it's just a name.**

---

### Global scope namespace

Global identifiers and named functions

#### com

##### com.mydomain

identifiers that refer to the functions and values used by your scripts

##### com.otherdomain

identifiers that refer to the functions and values defined by 3rd party scripts that are attached to your page. The have their own namespace so won't crash with your names.

---

**Above:** JavaScript simulates namespaces using objects. Reversing your domain name is the best way to ensure your names don't clash with others'.

## Creating a Namespace

Let's create a namespace for the objects in our Simple Quiz project.

1. Open quizQuestions.js in your editor and create a couple of empty lines at the top of the document.

2. We're going to use `com.flametreepublishing` as our namespace – this means we need to create an object called `com` inside the global namespace and another called `flametreepublishing` inside the `com` object.

```
1  var com;
2  if(!com) {
3      com = {};
4  }
5  if(!com.flametreepublishing) {
6      com.flametreepublishing = {};
7  }
```

**Above:** Step 3: Copy the code shown here into your editor.

3. Copy the code shown in the illustration (right). After declaring – but not initializing – `com`, we test that each namespace object does not exist before initializing it (see Logical NOT Operator, page 57). This is to avoid initializing an existing namespace.

4. Now we'll adapt the rest of the script so that it uses the new namespace – see the un-dimmed sections of the illustration, right.

```
9  com.flametreepublishing.questions = [];
10
11 //QUESTION 1
12 com.flametreepublishing.questions.push({
13     question: "Approximately how far away from the Earth is the Sun?",
14     answers: ["200 miles", "93,000,000 miles", "49,000,000 miles", "150,000 miles"],
15     correctAnswerIndex: 1}
16 );
17
18 //QUESTION 2
19 com.flametreepublishing.questions.push({
20     question: "How many planets are there in our solar system?",
21     answers: ["6", "7", "8", "9"],
22     correctAnswerIndex: 2}
23 );
24
25 //QUESTION 3
26 com.flametreepublishing.questions.push({
27     question: "Which of these is a moon of Jupiter?",
28     answers: ["Ganymede", "Miranda", "Enceladus", "Mars"],
```

**Above:** Step 4: Adapt the script as highlighted here.

5. Save quizQuestions.js and open quizFunctions.js. It is good practice to include your namespace declaration at the top of all scripts, so copy it to the top of quizFunctions.js.

```
 9  com.flametreepublishing.renderQuestionAtIndex = function(questionIndex) {
10      document.write("<h2>QUESTION " + (questionIndex + 1) + "</h2>");
11      var questionObject = com.flametreepublishing.questions[questionIndex];
12      document.write("<p>" + questionObject.question + "</p>");
13      document.write("<p>A1: " + questionObject.answers[0] + "</p>");
14      document.write("<p>A2: " + questionObject.answers[1] + "</p>");
15      document.write("<p>A3: " + questionObject.answers[2] + "</p>");
16      document.write("<p>A4: " + questionObject.answers[3] + "</p>");
17  }
18
19  com.flametreepublishing.checkUserAnswer = function(questionIndex, answerIndex) {
20      var questionObject = com.flametreepublishing.questions[questionIndex];
21      var theResult;
```

**Above:** Step 6: Update the references as highlighted here.

6. In order to place the functions within our namespace, we need to change them to anonymous functions. We also need to update all references to the questions array – see the highlighted portions of the illustration above.

7. Save the document and then open simpleQuiz.html in your editor. Locate the for loop and update its condition expression and function call, as shown in the illustration below.

```
12          <script type="text/javascript">
13              for(var i = 0; i < com.flametreepublishing.questions.length ; i++) {
14                  com.flametreepublishing.renderQuestionAtIndex(i);
15              }
16          </script>
```

**Above:** Step 7: Update the condition expression and function call as shown here.

8. Save your work and open the page in Firefox – again, it should look identical to previously, but underneath we have a pristine and unpolluted namespace.

# OBJECT ORIENTED PROGRAMMING

Object oriented programming – OOP – is an approach to programming that places objects at the heart of everything. While JavaScript is not a true OOP language, because it lacks specific constructs that are requirements for true OOP, it can be – and normally is – used in an OOP style.

## WHY USE OOP TECHNIQUES?

Far too many words have been written by others about the relative merits and drawbacks of OOP compared to other approaches to programming – and we're not going to add to them. Suffice it to say that one of the most compelling features of OOP is that it organizes things in much the same way as our human brains do. For this reason if no other, it is the most widely used approach to programming.

**Above:** OOP structures code in much the same way as humans structure thoughts.

# HOW WE CLASSIFY THINGS

When we think about a thing in the physical world, that thing is normally part of a family of similar things; this family is in turn part of a larger grouping, and so on. These groupings classify the thing we were thinking about in the first place.

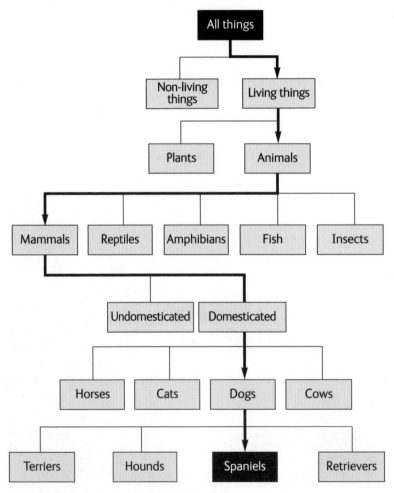

For example, we could classify a spaniel as a dog, as domesticated, as a mammal, as an animal, and as a living thing. This gives a chain of classification that defines something dog-like. Each point in that chain specifies characteristics that hone the definition – the number of legs an animal has, for instance, or the smoothness of a dog's fur.

With sufficient classification and definition of characteristics, we can determine that something is a spaniel as opposed to anything else in the entire universe; we do this without even thinking about it.

**Above:** By classifying things, we also define them.

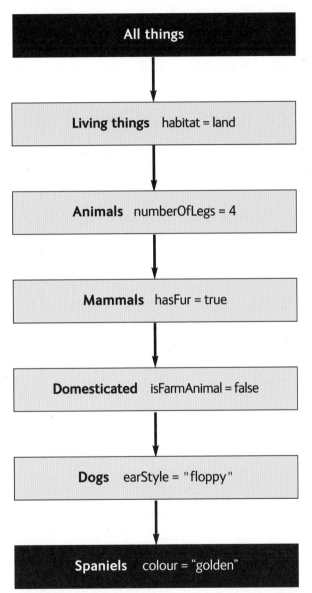

**Above:** In the physical world, characteristics are inherited and become an intrinsic part of a thing's definition – the same is true in OOP.

# CLASSES IN OOP

OOP harnesses exactly this system of hierarchical classification. We write scripts called **classes** that define **properties**. The properties describe the characteristics of – and are intrinsic to – the class. Classes also define **methods**, these being functions that operate on objects of the class.

A class inherits the properties and methods of its ancestor classes, taking on aspects of their characteristics and behaviour. This is much like a spaniel's inherent spaniel-ness being a function of the compounded characteristics and classifications it belongs to.

## Constructors and Instances

The code you write in a class script is like a template – it describes the properties and methods that define objects of that class.

However, this class definition is not an object of that class – to create one of those, we must call the class's **constructor** function, because it is this that generates an object from the class definition. This generated object is known as an **instance** of the class, so the act of calling the class constructor is often referred to as **instantiating** the class.

## A Massive Topic

OOP is a very deep subject that we aren't going to delve into – if it's something you want to explore, Google 'OOP' and take your pick from the thousands of results.
What we are going to do, though, is find out how to create and use basic custom classes in JavaScript.

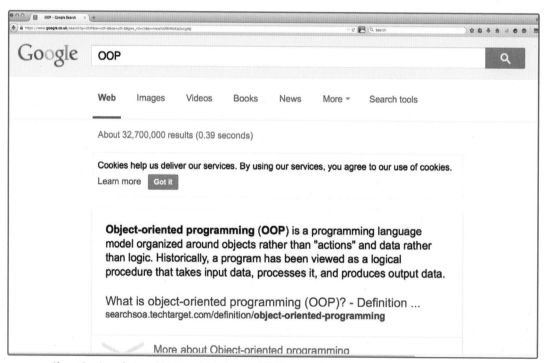

**Above:** Google can find over 33 million articles relating to OOP. That's an awful lot of reading.

# JAVASCRIPT CLASSES

We've already been working with JavaScript classes – number, string and array are all built-in classes. They all inherit some of their characteristics from the object class – in OOP parlance, this makes the object the **superclass** of those other classes.

We've also been working with class methods; for example, `write` is a method of the HTMLDocument class – we've used it as `document.write()`. (`document` is an instance of the HTMLDocument class.) These classes are built into the language, but we can also build our own.

## Defining a Custom Class

The questions in our Simple Quiz application are currently defined in generic objects – let's develop a QuizQuestion class instead.

1.  Create a new JavaScript document and save it in your Simple Quiz's js folder as QuizQuestion.js. Also create a `<script>` element in the `<head>` of simpleQuiz.html and link it to this new script. See the illustration below.

```
1   <!DOCTYPE HTML>
2   <html>
3       <head>
4           <title>A Simple Quiz</title>
5
6           <script type="text/javascript" src="js/QuizQuestion.js"></script>
7           <script type="text/javascript" src="js/quizQuestions.js"></script>
8           <script type="text/javascript" src="js/quizFunctions.js"></script>
9
10      </head>
11
12      <body>
13          <script type="text/javascript">
14              for(var i = 0; i < com.flametreepublishing.questions.length ; i++)
15                  com.flametreepublishing.renderQuestionAtIndex(i);
```

**Above:** Step 1: Create a new JavaScript document as shown here.

2. Add our namespace declaration at the top of QuizQuestion.js (*see* page 93).

3. We're going to call this class QuizQuestion, so the first thing to do is define the constructor function – see the illustration below. The constructor function has the same name as the class.

```
 1  var com;
 2  if(!com) {
 3      com = {};
 4  }
 5  if(!com.flametreepublishing) {
 6      com.flametreepublishing = {};
 7  }
 8
 9  com.flametreepublishing.QuizQuestion = function(aQuestionNum, aQuestionText, aAnswers, aCorrectAnswerIndex) {
10
11  }
```

**Above:** Step 3: Define the constructor function as shown here.

4. As you see, the constructor expects four parameters. These correspond to the properties we want QuizQuestion instances to have; we've added a leading 'a' to the names so they are distinct from the similarly named class properties.

5. Add the code highlighted in the illustration above to the body of the constructor.

```
 9  com.flametreepublishing.QuizQuestion = function(aQuestionNum,
10                                                  aQuestionText,
11                                                  aAnswers,
12                                                  aCorrectAnswerIndex) {
13      this.questionNum = aQuestionNum;
14      this.questionText = aQuestionText;
15      this.answers = aAnswers;
16      this.correctAnswerIndex = aCorrectAnswerIndex;
17  }
18
```

**Above:** Step 5: Add the code highlighted here.

Here, we meet the `this` keyword for the first time – see above.

6. Save your work.

# CREATING AN INSTANCE

Now that the constructor is defined, we can create a QuizQuestion instance by using the new keyword, like this:

```
new com.flametreepublishing.QuizQuestion(arguments);
```

Recall that the QuizQuestion constructor function expects four arguments to be passed to it: the question number, the question text, the array of possible answers, and the index of the correct answer. These all need to be included within the parentheses following the constructor name when instantiating the class – we'll come back to this shortly.

## Hot Tip

By convention, we name classes with a leading upper-case character, and instances with a leading lower-case character.

```
20    new com.flametreepublishing.QuizQuestion(
21        1,
22        "Approximately how far away from the Earth is the Sun?",
23        ["200 miles", "93,000,000 miles", "49,000,000 miles", "150,000 miles"],
24        1
25    )
26
```

**Above**: Instantiating a class creates an object of that class which we can then work with.

# THE THIS KEYWORD

The last walkthrough introduced the special this keyword. When used in a constructor function, this refers to the instance that's under construction.

In the code we've just written, there are four statements starting with this – these assign the argument values sent to the constructor to the new instance. By assigning these values to this, we assign them to the new instance.

When `this` is used in a class method, it refers to the specific instance of the class that the method is being executed on. This will become clearer over the coming exercises.

## CLASS METHODS

A method is similar to a function. In simple terms, where a function is a stand alone entity that can have objects passed to it, a method is part and parcel of an object, and operates from the context of that object.

We've already met a few methods of the built-in classes – for example, the `push()` method of the array class. When we call `push()`, we do so via an instance of the array class: `myArray.push(newValue)`, hence it is a method.

## The Prototype Object

As has been mentioned previously, the JavaScript object class holds an exalted place within the language – it is the class upon which all other classes are based. The upshot is that all other classes, including our own custom classes, inherit the methods and properties of the object class. One such property is called prototype – this is where the methods of a class should be defined. Let's see how.

```
25
26  //QUESTION 1
27  com.flametreepublishing.questions.push({
28      question: "Approximately how far away from the Earth is the Sun?",
29      answers: ["200 miles", "93,000,000 miles", "49,000,000 miles", "150,000 miles"],
30      correctAnswerIndex: 1}
31  );
32
```

**Above:** We've already met the push() method of the array class (note that com.flametreepublishing.questions is an instance of the array class).

## Defining Class Methods

We currently have a function in our quiz, checkUserAnswer, which would be better as a method of our new QuizQuestion class.

1.  Open QuizQuestion.js in your editor.

```
15
16  com.flametreepublishing.QuizQuestion.prototype.checkUserAnswer = function(answerIndex) {
17      var theResult;
18      if(answerIndex == this.correctAnswerIndex) {
19          theResult = true;
20      } else {
21          theResult = false;
22      }
23      return(theResult);
24  }
```

**Above:** Step 2: Insert the method definition as shown here.

2. Create a couple of empty lines below the constructor and then type the
`checkUserAnswer` method definition shown in the illustration on the previous page.
This uses much the same logic as our earlier function of the same name.

3. Note that the method name has to be prefixed by the namespace, the class name,
and the `prototype` property reference. This can become somewhat long-winded,
but is unavoidable.

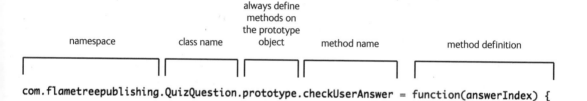

```
com.flametreepublishing.QuizQuestion.prototype.checkUserAnswer = function(answerIndex) {
```

**Above:** Method names can become a bit long-winded, but they have a simple structure.

4. While we're here, let's make the question self-rendering. The code for this is shown in the
illustration below and should be familiar by now.

5. Save your work.

```
26
27  com.flametreepublishing.QuizQuestion.prototype.renderQuestion = function() {
28      document.write("<h2>QUESTION " + this.questionNum + "</h2>");
29      document.write("<p>" + this.questionText + "</p>");
30      document.write("<p>A1: " + this.answers[0] + "</p>");
31      document.write("<p>A2: " + this.answers[1] + "</p>");
32      document.write("<p>A3: " + this.answers[2] + "</p>");
33      document.write("<p>A4: " + this.answers[3] + "</p>");
34  }
35
```

**Above:** Step 4: The code here will make the question self-rendering.

# CREATING A MAIN CLASS

When building a JavaScript application, it is common to create a main or central class in which to define properties and methods that are global to the application. The idea is that we create a single instance of this class, and use this as the central kicking-off and reference point for everything else in the application.

## A SimpleQuiz Class

Let's create a main class for our Simple Quiz application.

1. Create a new JavaScript document and save it in the project's js folder as SimpleQuiz.js.

2. Open simpleQuiz.html in your editor. Add a `<script>` element that links to the new SimpleQuiz.js script, and delete the `<script>` elements that link to quizQuestions.js and quizFunctions.js. Save the HTML file and switch back to SimpleQuiz.js. See the illustration, right.

```
1  <!DOCTYPE HTML>
2  <html>
3      <head>
4          <title>A Simple Quiz</title>
5
6          <script type="text/javascript" src="js/QuizQuestion.js"></script>
7          <script type="text/javascript" src="js/SimpleQuiz.js"></script>
8
9      </head>
```

**Above**: Step 2: Add the code as shown here.

3. Add our standard namespace declaration and create a constructor function – see the illustration, right.

```
1  var com;
2  if(!com) {
3      com = {};
4  }
5  if(!com.flametreepublishing) {
6      com.flametreepublishing = {};
7  }
8
9  com.flametreepublishing.SimpleQuiz = function() {
10
11 }
```

**Above**: Step 3: Create a constructor function as shown here.

4. We still need an array in which to store the QuizQuestion objects – we'll make this a property of the SimpleQuiz class by declaring and initializing it in the constructor as shown in the illustration, right.

```
8
9  com.flametreepublishing.SimpleQuiz = function() {
10     this.questions = [];
11 }
12
```

**Above**: Step 4: Declare and initialize the array as shown here.

```
 9  com.flametreepublishing.SimpleQuiz = function() {
10      this.questions = [];
11      this.loadQuestions();
12  }
13
14  com.flametreepublishing.SimpleQuiz.prototype.loadQuestions = function() {
15      //QUESTION 1
16      this.questions.push(
17          new com.flametreepublishing.QuizQuestion(
18              1,
19              "Approximately how far away from the Earth is the Sun?",
20              ["200 miles", "93,000,000 miles", "49,000,000 miles", "150,000 miles"],
21              1
22          )
23      );
24      //QUESTION 2
25      this.questions.push(
26          new com.flametreepublishing.QuizQuestion(
27              2,
28              "How many planets are there in our Solar System?",
```

**Above:** Steps 5 & 6: Add a call to loadQuestions(), as shown here.

5.  In a completed quiz application, we might download the question data from a web server, but for simplicity, we're going to hard-code the questions into our SimpleQuiz class. We'll simulate a download by calling the method loadQuestions() – see the illustration above.

6.  In the constructor, add a call to loadQuestions(), as in the illustration above. Notice that we do this through the this keyword.

7.  SimpleQuiz can now load and store QuizQuestion objects, but we no longer have a way to render all questions (consider that QuizQuestion's renderQuestion method needs to be called from somewhere).

8.  Create a new method of SimpleQuiz called renderAllQuestions().

```
44  com.flametreepublishing.SimpleQuiz.prototype.renderAllQuestions = function() {
45      for(var i = 0; i < this.questions.length; i++) {
46          this.questions[i].renderQuestion();
47      }
48  }
```

**Above:** Steps 7, 8 & 9: This is how to render all questions, as described in the steps above.

9.  Within the body of `renderAllQuestions`, create a `for` loop that calls `renderQuestion()` on each QuizQuestion object as in the illustration.

10. Save SimpleQuiz.js and switch to simpleQuiz.html.

```
11      <body>
12          <script type="text/javascript">
13              com.flametreepublishing.simpleQuiz = new com.flametreepublishing.SimpleQuiz();
14          </script>
15
16      </body>
```

**Above:** Steps 10, 11 & 12: In these steps, you will instantiate SimpleQuiz.

11. Locate the `<script>` element that's within the `<body>` element, and delete the `for` loop – it's now obsolete.

12. Within the same `<script>` block, instantiate SimpleQuiz and assign the instance to `com.flametreepublishing.simpleQuiz`, as shown in the illustration above.

13. Finally, call `renderAllQuestions()` on the newly created SimpleQuiz object as shown below.

```
11
12          <script type="text/javascript">
13              com.flametreepublishing.simpleQuiz = new com.flametreepublishing.SimpleQuiz();
14              com.flametreepublishing.simpleQuiz.renderAllQuestions();
15          </script>
16
```

**Above:** Step 13: Ensure your HTML page looks like this!

14. Save and close all open files. If you open the page in your browser, nothing will have changed visually, all being well.

THE DOM & EVENTS

# WORKING WITH THE DOM

Every script we've written so far has worked by outputting data to the page while the page loads. This is OK – but limiting. What if we want to manipulate the page after it has loaded? How do we achieve this?

## DYNAMIC HTML

All major browsers support something called Dynamic HTML – or DHTML for short. DHTML allows JavaScript to make changes to a page after it has been loaded and rendered in the browser, with such changes immediately shown on screen. This presents us with a whole host of possibilities – your imagination really is the limit.

```
22
23  /*-------------------------------------------------------------------
24  We've changed checkUserAnswer() considerably - see comments within the body of the
25  method...
26  --------------------------------------------------------------------*/
27  com.flametreepublishing.QuizQuestion.prototype.checkUserAnswer = function(answerIndex) {
28      //Initialise theResult to false - we can change this if the question was correctly answered
29      var theResult = false;
30      if(this.questionAnswered) {
31          //If the question has already been answered then report this in an alert and do nothing more
32          alert("You've already answered this question");
33      } else if(answerIndex == this.correctAnswerIndex) {
34          //If the correct answer is given then mark the question as being correctly answered
35          this.answeredCorrectly = true;
36          //Now set the style class of the question's <div> so that it changes to green
37          document.getElementById("q" + this.questionNum).className = "correctlyAnswered";
38          //And set theResult to true
39          theResult = true;
40      } else {
41          //If the question has been incorrectly answered then change the <div> style class name
42          //so that it has a red background
43          document.getElementById("q" + this.questionNum).className = "incorrectlyAnswered";
44      }
45      //Record that this question has now been answered
46      this.questionAnswered = true;
47      //Now return the result. This isn't actually being used any more, but it's nonetheless
48      //useful to have methods return a result, even if only to indicate that the code was
49      //executed in full without errors.
50      return(theResult);
```

**Above:** Additional explanations are contained in the downloadable code examples.

## Hot Tip

**Be sure to download the code examples – see page 7. As well as enabling you to check your code against ours, you'll also find comments included that help to further explain the examples.**

# HTML IS HIERARCHICAL

All HTML documents contain an `<html>` element; this element always contains a `<head>` and a `<body>` element; these elements themselves contain other elements. A page is, therefore, a hierarchical structure of HTML elements. We express this structure in terms of ancestry: `<html>` is the **root** and has two **children**, `<head>` and `<body>`; `<html>` is the **parent** of `<head>` and `<body>`; `<head>` and `<body>` are **siblings**.

## What is the DOM?

We know that JavaScript enables us to create similar hierarchical structures by storing objects within other objects; as it turns out, this is exactly how a web page is represented under the hood of the browser. This representation – or model – is known as the Document Object Model, or DOM for short.

```
<html>
    <head>
        <title>
            A Simple Quiz
        </title>
        <script>
            js/SimpleQuiz.js
        </script>
    </head>

    <body>
        <h3>
            A Simple Quiz
        </h3>
        <div>
            <h3>
                Question 1
            </h3>
            etc.
        </div>
    </body>
</html>
```

**Above:** HTML elements are nested within other HTML elements; all elements have a parent, and many have siblings and children.

# DOM PROGRAMMING

JavaScript's DOM classes, such as HTMLDocument and HTMLElement, provide numerous methods for manipulating a loaded page, and expose properties that directly map to HTML attributes. For example, a <p> element is represented in the DOM by an HTMLElement object. Any attributes defined on the <p> element are available to JavaScript as properties of the corresponding object; any properties defined by JavaScript on the object become attribute values of the <p> element.

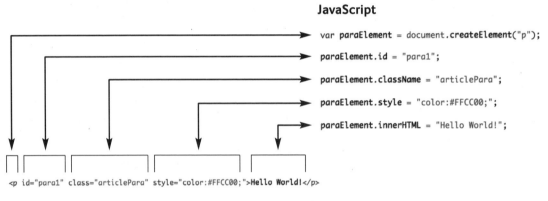

**JavaScript**

```
var paraElement = document.createElement("p");
paraElement.id = "para1";
paraElement.className = "articlePara";
paraElement.style = "color:#FFCC00;";
paraElement.innerHTML = "Hello World!";
```

```
<p id="para1" class="articlePara" style="color:#FFCC00;">Hello World!</p>
```

**HTML**

**Above:** Attributes of an HTML element become properties of the corresponding DOM object, and vice versa.

## Retrieving Elements from the DOM

As we've seen, all HTML elements (with the exception of <html>) have to be nested within another element. Therefore, to add a new element to a page with JavaScript, we often have to retrieve the element from the DOM that will serve as the parent of the new element. At other times, we may want to apply, say, a style change to all elements of a certain type.

The methods for getting elements are defined on the single HTMLDocument instance, the top level of the DOM. We have already been using this object in our scripts – every time we type document, we are accessing this HTMLDocument object.

## Adding Elements to the DOM

Let's explore DOM programming by updating the QuizQuestion class's renderQuestion method.

1. Open QuizQuestion.js in your editor and locate the renderQuestion method.

2. Currently, this method uses document.write to output a literal HTML string to the page. This technique only works if the method is executed while the page is loading – let's fix that.

```
36
37  com.flametreepublishing.QuizQuestion.prototype.renderQuestion = function() {
38      document.write("<h2>QUESTION " + this.questionNum + "</h2>");
39      document.write("<p>" + this.questionText + "</p>");
40      document.write("<p>A1: " + this.answers[0] + "</p>");
41      document.write("<p>A2: " + this.answers[1] + "</p>");
42      document.write("<p>A3: " + this.answers[2] + "</p>");
43      document.write("<p>A4: " + this.answers[3] + "</p>");
44  }
45
```

**Above:** This method won't work once the page has loaded.

3. Delete the body of the renderQuestion method.

4. On-screen, we're going to lay out each question inside a <div> element – the code in the illustration below shows you how to create one. Note that this new <div> is not yet part of the page – it's created off-screen, where it stays until it's assigned to a parent element.

```
36
37  com.flametreepublishing.QuizQuestion.prototype.renderQuestion = function() {
38      var questionDiv = document.createElement("div");
39
40  }
41
```

**Above:** Step 4: document.createElement() creates new elements off-screen.

```
36
37  com.flametreepublishing.QuizQuestion.prototype.renderQuestion = function() {
38      var questionDiv = document.createElement("div");
39      questionDiv.id = "q" + this.questionNum;
40      var questionHeading = document.createElement("h2");
41      questionHeading.innerHTML = "QUESTION " + this.questionNum;
42      questionDiv.appendChild(questionHeading);
43
44  }
```

**Above:** Steps 5 & 6: Continue to build the question's HTML elements, like this.

5. Give the <div> an id value derived from the QuizQuestion object's questionNum property as in line 39 of the illustration above.

6. We'll create an <h2> element to hold the question title; once created, we need to give it some text content using the HTMLElement object's innerHTML property, and add it to the <div> with appendChild – see the illustration above.

7. Use the same techniques to add the text for the question and answers to the <div>, as shown in the illustration below.

```
41      questionHeading.innerHTML = "QUESTION " + this.question
42      questionDiv.appendChild(questionHeading);
43      var questionTextPara = document.createElement("p");
44      questionTextPara.innerHTML = this.questionText;
45      questionDiv.appendChild(questionTextPara);
46      for(var i = 0; i < this.answers.length; i++) {
47          var answerPara = document.createElement("p");
48          answerPara.innerHTML = this.answers[i];
49          answerPara.id = "a" + i;
50          questionDiv.appendChild(answerPara);
51      }
52
53  }
```

**Above:** Steps 7 & 8: This code will build the rest of the HTML elements needed to display the question.

8. Notice that rather than manually typing code for each of the possible answers, we've wrapped this up in a `for` loop that iterates through the `answers` array. Also notice that we've set an `id` attribute for each answer's `<p>` element.

9. Finally, we need to add our `<div>` element to the page. We'll add it to the `<body>` element, which can be accessed with `document.body` as in the illustration below.

10. Save your work and open the page in Firefox. Once again, we see the same thing as before, but this time we have built the page using DOM programming.

```
49          answerPara.id = a + 1;
50          questionDiv.appendChild(answerPara);
51      }
52      document.body.appendChild(questionDiv);
53  }
54
```

**Above:** Step 9: Add the element to the page, as shown here.

# EVENTS

Web pages issue events in response to various conditions and user actions, such as a page having loaded successfully, or the user clicking on something. Responding to these events is one of JavaScript's key roles.

## JAVASCRIPT EVENT MODELS

There are a few different event models in JavaScript that have evolved over the years. We don't have space to cover them all, so we'll focus on the current best practice model, known as the W3C model. This isn't the simplest of the models, but it's the one that you should aim to use.

**Hot Tip**

If you want to explore all of the JavaScript event models, an excellent discussion of them can be found at www.quirksmode.org/js/introevents.html

**Left:** Quirksmode.org/js/ is a fantastic resource for both new and experienced JavaScript developers.

# WHAT IS AN EVENT?

An event is a message issued by the browser. An event always has a type – the type indicates the nature of the event – whether it's a click, a page load, a key press and so on. For example, clicking on any element in a page causes that element to send – or **dispatch** – an event of type `"click"`.

# LISTENING FOR AN EVENT

In order to respond to an event, we have to write code that 'listens' for that event occurring – this code is called an **event listener**. When an event listener detects an event of the type it is listening for, it evaluates an expression that performs some action(s) in response to the event.

**Above:** Events are generated by elements on a page; JavaScript can listen for those events.

## Event Handlers

Typically, when an event listener is triggered, the expression it executes is a function or method call. The function or method being called is referred to as an event **handler**. It is the event handler's job to deal with the event in some way – making visual changes, sending data to a server, and so on.

## Adding an Event Handler

Our Simple Quiz application needs to be able to respond to the user clicking on an answer – let's define an event handler as a first step.

1. Open SimpleQuiz.js. We're going to create a new method called clickHandler – move to the bottom of the document and add the method as shown in the illustration below.

```
59
60  com.flametreepublishing.SimpleQuiz.prototype.clickHandler = function(e) {
61      //click handler statements go here
62  }
63
64
```

**Above:** Step 1: Add the method as shown here.

2. When using the W3C event model, the event handler is always passed an object containing details about the event – our method captures this as the parameter e. By doing this, we can access the element on which the event occurred by referencing e.target as in the illustration below.

```
59
60  com.flametreepublishing.SimpleQuiz.prototype.clickHandler = function(e) {
61      var clickedAnswerId = e.target.id;
62  }
63
```

**Above:** Step 2: e.target references the HTML element that triggered the event.

3. We need to identify the answer that was clicked – this is why our code defines an id value for each answer's <p> element. Each answer's id is the answer index prefixed by the letter

```
59
60  com.flametreepublishing.SimpleQuiz.prototype.clickHandler = function(e) {
61      var clickedAnswerId = e.target.id;
62      var clickedAnswerIndex = Number(clickedAnswerId.substr(1, 1));
63  }
64
```

**Above**: Step 3: This code identifies which answer has been clicked.

'a', so we need to access just the second character of the id; we cast this second character to a number because we are going to use it as an index of the questions array. See the illustration above.

4. Note the use of the substr() method of the string class, which enables us to access a section of the string it is called on. The first parameter is the character position that the section starts on (zero-based, like an array index); the second is the length of the section to return.

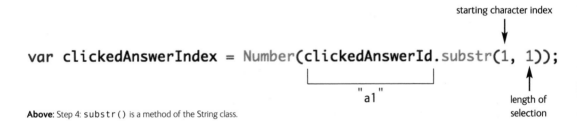

**Above**: Step 4: substr() is a method of the String class.

5. Our event handler also needs to know the question number – we can extract this from the <div> element's id attribute. We can access the <div> by referencing e.target.parentNode (the <div> is the parent of the <p>) as in the illustration below.

```
62      var clickedAnswerIndex = Number(clickedAnswerId.substr(1, 1));
63      var clickedQuestionId = e.target.parentNode.id;
64      var clickedQuestionNum = Number(clickedQuestionId.substr(1, 1));
65  }
66
```

**Above**: Step 5: Extract the question number that has been answered from the event object.

**6.** Now the handler knows the question number, it can retrieve the corresponding QuizQuestion object from the `questions` array. However, in an event handler, `this` refers to the element that triggered the event, not the object handling the event, so we need to use a global reference to access the `questions` array. The code for this is in the illustration below.

> ## Hot Tip
>
> The `parentNode` property of an HTML element refers to the parent of that element, i.e. the element in which an element is nested.

```
59
60  com.flametreepublishing.SimpleQuiz.prototype.clickHandler = function(e) {
61      var clickedAnswerId = e.target.id;
62      var clickedAnswerIndex = Number(clickedAnswerId.substr(1, 1));
63      var clickedQuestionId = e.target.parentNode.id;
64      var clickedQuestionNum = Number(clickedQuestionId.substr(1, 1));
65      var clickedQuestion = com.flametreepublishing.simpleQuiz.questions[clickedQuestionNum -1];
66  }
67
```

**Above:** Step 6: This code retrieves the QuizQuestion object for the answer that was clicked.

**7.** Now that we have the QuizQuestion object and answer index that the user clicked, we can determine whether the correct answer was given and report this to the user – this code is shown in the illustration below.

```
65      var clickedQuestion = com.flametreepublishing.simpleQuiz.questions
66      if(clickedQuestion.checkUserAnswer(clickedAnswerIndex)) {
67          alert("Correct! Well done.");
68      } else {
69          alert("No - that's not correct. Try again.");
70      }
71  }
```

**Above:** Step 7: The code given here will inform the user whether or not their answer was correct.

**8.** Save your work. Don't open the file in your browser yet – we're not quite finished.

## EVENT LISTENERS

Event listeners are assigned to the object that generates the event we want to capture – often this is a DOM object from the web page. Once we know the object we want to listen to, we call `addEventListener()` on that object – the general form is:

`myObject.addEventListener(`*eventType, handlerExpression, useCapture*`)`

## Parameters of the AddEventListener() Method

○ **Event type:** The first parameter indicates the type of event to listen for. This is a string such as `"click"`, `"keydown"` or `"mouseover"`.

○ **Handler expression:** Typically a reference to a handler function or method. Note that when referencing a function or method, we do not include parentheses.

○ **Use capture:** This is complex and beyond the scope of the book. Until you learn what this does, always pass `false` to this parameter.

```
1
2  function clickHandler() {
3       //do things in response to the click
4  }
5
6  var myPara = document.createElement("p");
7  document.body.appendChild(myPara);
8  myPara.addEventListener("click", clickHandler, false);
9
```

**Above:** Adding an event listener to a `<p>` element.

## Adding Event Listeners

We've created our event handler, but it doesn't do anything until triggered by an event listener.

1. Open QuizQuestion.js and locate the `for` loop within the `renderQuestion` method.

```
46    for(var i = 0; i < this.answers.length; i++) {
47        var answerPara = document.createElement("p");
48        answerPara.innerHTML = this.answers[i];
49        answerPara.id = "a" + i;
50        answerPara.addEventListener("click", com.flametreepublishing.simpleQuiz.clickHandler, false);
51        questionDiv.appendChild(answerPara);
52    }
```

**Above:** Step 2: Enter the code shown here as described above.

2. Create an empty line after the one that sets the `answerPara.id` property and insert the code shown in the illustration on the previous page.

3. We don't include the parentheses in the reference to the handler method. If we did, the expression would be evaluated as a method call when the event listener is assigned – we want the expression to be the name of the handler, not a call to it.

4. Save your work, open simpleQuiz.html in Firefox and click an answer. At last – we have a working quiz.

**Above:** After all our hard work, we have a functioning quiz.

## FINISHING TOUCHES

Let's add one more event listener and handler – they will start the application when the page load completes.

1. Create a new JavaScript document and save it in your project's js folder as quizStartup.js. Enter our namespace declaration at the top of the document.

2. Add the event handler code shown in the illustration on the next page. You should understand it by now – if not, download our code examples and study the comments.

```
 8
 9 com.flametreepublishing.startQuiz = function() {
10     com.flametreepublishing.simpleQuiz = new com.flametreepublishing.SimpleQuiz();
11     com.flametreepublishing.simpleQuiz.renderAllQuestions();
12 }
13
```

**Above:** Step 2: The event handler code.

3. Add the event listener code shown in the illustration below. The `window` object represents the browser window – we're listening for its `load` event, dispatched when the page has finished loading.

```
11         com.flametreepublishing.simpleQuiz.renderAllQuestions();
12 }
13
14 window.addEventListener("load", com.flametreepublishing.startQuiz, false);
15
```

**Above:** Step 3: The event listener code.

4. Save your work and open simpleQuiz.html in your editor.

5. Add a new `<script>` element in the `<head>` and link it to quizStartup.js. Then delete the `<script>` element that's within the `<body>` element entirely, and save the file. See the illustration, below.

```
 3     <head>
 4         <title>A Simple Quiz</title>
 5
 6         <script type="text/javascript" src="js/QuizQuestion.js"></script>
 7         <script type="text/javascript" src="js/SimpleQuiz.js"></script>
 8         <script type="text/javascript" src="js/quizStartup.js"></script>
 9
10     </head>
```

**Above:** Step 5: Ensure you add and delete the right code here.

### Next Steps

And that's it – our quiz now works! More to the point, consider what our HTML document contains: just three script elements. JavaScript is handling everything else – nice!

If you want to improve on the quiz game, why not add a style sheet to make things look prettier? You could also take it up a level by recording the user's answers and tracking their score – you have the knowledge to do this. For additional tips though, see SimpleQuiz_onwards in the code examples package.

## ONWARDS!

You've taken your first steps into the deep and detailed world of JavaScript. You should feel that you have gained a solid overview of the language and how to use it, but there's still much more to learn...

Happy coding!

**Above:** Try improving the quiz with some CSS and new functionality. Pack it full of your own questions and test your friends and family.

# ONLINE RESOURCES

## USEFUL WEBSITES

**Mozilla Developer Network (MDN)**: This site provides all the nitty-gritty detail of the languages supported by Firefox, and how it works with them. A visit to the JavaScript section provides guides, tutorials, an object and class reference section, and more. developer.mozilla.org

**The JavaScript Source:** This site provides a whole host of code snippets that you can copy, paste and adapt into your own code – and they're all free. Why re-invent the wheel when you can download one somebody already made! javascriptsource.com

**How To Node:** If you want to start exploring server-side JavaScript then How To Node is a great resource, full of information and tutorials. howtonode.org

## FURTHER READING

Crute, A., *Coding HTML and CSS*, Flame Tree Publishing, 2015

Flanagan, D., *JavaScript: The Definitive Guide*, O'Reilly Media, 2011. Widely considered to be the bible of JavaScript, this book covers all aspects of the language in intricate detail, yet maintains an engaging and accessible style throughout. The book includes a comprehensive reference section describing the properties and methods of all built-in objects and classes.

Zakas, N. C., *The Principles of Object-Oriented JavaScript*, No Starch Press, 2014. The author explores JavaScript, unlocking some of the deepest secrets of the language's inner workings along the way.

Powers, S., *JavaScript Cookbook*, O'Reilly Media, 2015: This book is packed with practical code examples. It is aimed at JavaScript developers with some experience, the 'recipes' cover a wide range of scenarios, and offer fast-track solutions to many coding conundrums.

# INDEX